Arts-Based Thought Experiments for a Posthuman Earth

Imagination and Praxis: Criticality and Creativity in Education and Educational Research

VOLUME 16

The titles published in this series are listed at *brill.com/ipcc*

Arts-Based Thought Experiments for a Posthuman Earth

A Touchstones Companion

Edited by

Alexandra Lasczik and Amy Cutter-Mackenzie-Knowles

BRILL

LEIDEN | BOSTON

All chapters in this book have undergone peer review.

Library of Congress Cataloging-in-Publication Data

Names: Cutcher, Alexandra J., editor. | Cutter-Mackenzie, Amy, editor.
Title: Arts-based thought experiments for a posthuman Earth : a Touchstones companion / edited by Alexandra Lasczik and Amy Cutter-Mackenzie-Knowles.
Other titles: Touchstones for deterritorializing socioecological learning.
Description: Leiden ; Boston : Brill, [2022] | Series: Imagination and praxis : criticality and creativity in education and educational research, 2542-9140 ; volume 16 | Includes bibliographical references and index.
Identifiers: LCCN 2021060320 (print) | LCCN 2021060321 (ebook) | ISBN 9789004507814 (paperback) | ISBN 9789004507821 (hardback) | ISBN 9789004507838 (ebook)
Subjects: LCSH: Thought experiments. | Arts in education.
Classification: LCC BD265 .A78 202 (print) | LCC BD265 (ebook) | DDC 100--dc23/eng/20211220
LC record available at https://lccn.loc.gov/2021060320
LC ebook record available at https://lccn.loc.gov/2021060321

Typeface for the Latin, Greek, and Cyrillic scripts: “Brill”. See and download: brill.com/brill-typeface.

ISSN 2542-9140
ISBN 978-90-04-50781-4 (paperback)
ISBN 978-90-04-50782-1 (hardback)
ISBN 978-90-04-50783-8 (e-book)

This book is printed on acid-free paper and produced in a sustainable manner.

For the posthuman Earth to come

Contents

Foreword

When I was invited to write the Foreword for this remarkable book, I knew I was in for a treat, but I didn't fully appreciate the gift it would be. I have known both editors and some of the authors for a number of years, and have spent time with many of them at Southern Cross University. The editors and I share commitments within other projects, so I am very aware of their work in education. With that said, as I read the book, I gradually came to more fully appreciate the community of practice that the book represents. Moreover, I came to appreciate the profound sense of reciprocity that permeates everything about the way this book is conceived, enlivened and enacted. I feel like I received it as a gift from friends and colleagues, and I can feel that the process of imagining and creating the book was also a circulation of gifts among these friends and colleagues.

I want to pause for a moment and think about gifts and how this book is a gift. Settlers aligned with the modern West (minority world) have often understood gifts as individually defined and offered as a token of affection without expectations. This conception is aligned with a strong sense of individualism and often given as a purchased commodity. Many Indigenous cultures understand gifts from a collective point-of-view, where systems of social exchange create forms of sociality that recognise a collective indebtedness: gifts are given and gifts are returned. In this reciprocity, there is a certainty to the continuation of culture as well as relations within the culture. There are still other cultures and groups around the world that understand the reciprocity of gifts between these conceptions, where there is not an obligation, and the spirit of the gift may be received individually or collectively. Within these and other conceptions there is an understanding of how people relate to one another as well as how they relate to and through non-human things. Without turning this foreword into a scholarly essay on gift giving, I will say that many scholars study gift exchange across the world. That is not my intention here. Instead, I want to posit that it is a generous gift for its commitment to intellectual exchange through creative and critical experiments. It also demonstrates a very different conception of how artist-scholars-educators can be committed to being in, of and through the world, and ultimately, how they exchange gifts within their circles.

This book is uniquely created as an arts-based companion to a richly conceptual book entitled *Touchstones for Deterritorializing Socioecological Learning: The Anthropocene, Posthumanism and Common Worlds as Creative*

Milieux. While the first book is a complex and highly theoretical offering to the field of education and particularly to socioecological learning through the touchstones of the Anthropocene, posthumanism and common worlds through creative milieux, this companion text creatively engages with the content in the first by pursuing arts-based thought experiments as the authors worked the touchstones. The result is a richly evocative and provocative text that is utterly innovative in the field.

The exchanges in this book feel like gifts as they are abundantly rich in creative experimentation, shifting our attention from standard academic prose to narratives, scripts, found poems, and visual collages. These exchanges invite us to perceive the world differently, living alongside our ecological roots as well as our humanly concerns. These exchanges gift us with demonstrations of qualitatively different engagements, offering us openings to new ways of receiving the world and in turn new ways of being in and of the world. It also offers us demonstrations of how we might give back to the world, of how we may offer gifts to the world. It disrupts how the academy interacts within itself as well as with society. We are eager to receive these extraordinary gifts and I know we will be inspired to return even more by circulating what we imagine within other circles closer to home or perhaps further afield.

One of the most unique premises of this book is its relationship with the first scholarly text and thus its commitment to companionship. There is an inherent relational nature to each offering that thinks alongside the first text, as a companion. There are also the authorial relations within each chapter and simultaneously with all of the authors in the book: they too are companions creatively engaging with the touchstones. This network of relations was skilfully arranged through retreats where the collective of authors read, wrote, created and discussed a range of concepts as a community of inquirers. The authors were intellectual, physical and creative companions gifting one another and us with demonstrations of deterritorializing socioecological learning. The power of this book is not only in the companionship between these two independent texts, it is rooted in the creative thinking alongside that gifts us with powerful new insights and understandings, and I would say, ways of being with and alongside one another. It also gifts us an opportunity to witness what we are able to do collectively when we take up timely yet challenging ideas, and pursue them individually and together. Witnessing this work is a gift. We can immediately understand how we could enact these challenging ideas. What a gift. Through the power of expression, imagination and the creative milieux, we are able to see the world anew, differently and diffractively. Such a profound gift.

As I draw this to a close, I wish to thank editors Alexandra Lasczik and Amy Cutter-Mackenzie-Knowles, and all of the authors, for their commitment to embodying and enacting the touchstones. Readers will be forever grateful.

This book is pure gift. Thank you.

Rita L. Irwin
Distinguished University Scholar
Professor, Art Education
The University of British Columbia, Vancouver, Canada

Acknowledgements

In the first instance, we would like to acknowledge the Bundjalung Country of the Arakwal people upon which much of this work was completed. We pay our respects to the traditional custodians of the land and Elders past and present, who have cared for that Country for thousands of generations. We recognise that sovereignty was never ceded, and that this Country always was and always will be, Aboriginal land. We are grateful to be able to live and work here.

We would also like to recognise the support of the Faculty of Education at Southern Cross University, Australia, specifically in their funding of the writing retreats that make the development of such collections possible. In particular, we acknowledge the support of the Sustainability, Environment and the Arts in Education (SEAE) Research Cluster and its members for their enduring support of our projects and each other. It is a unique community of practice.

Thanks also goes to Katie Hotko, who has worked diligently and with constant good humour to support the assembling of this book, and who also opened the doors of Diptipur to all in the SEAE Research Cluster.

Reviewer List

We would like to thank our wonderful reviewers who took precious time out of their busy work lives to evaluate the chapters of this collection during the pandemic. Their unseen labour ought not go unrecognised and so we list them here, with grateful thanks:

Ali Black
Adrienne Boulton
Pamela Burnard
Melisa Cahnmann-Taylor
Trish Osler
Michaela Pegum
David Rousell
Nuper Sachdeva
Debbie Smith-Shank
Valerie Triggs
Bronwen Wade-Leeuwen
Richard Saunders White

Notes on Contributors

Raoul Adam
is a senior lecturer at Southern Cross University. He has over twenty-five years of experience in education as a senior secondary school teacher and senior university lecturer in educational philosophy and psychology. His research relates to education for wicked problems and the interaction between different ways of knowing and being in complex and contested spaces. Raoul has designed and delivered over 20 units across three universities in fields including, Educational Psychology, Educational Philosophy, Interdisciplinary Studies, Philosophy of Religion, Research Methods, Pedagogy, and Curriculum Studies. He has also led projects in Design Thinking and Critical & Creative Thinking, and Metacognition. Raoul also developed curriculum frameworks for UNESCO in Educational Philosophy and Educational Psychology. His current research focusses on the design and development of a digital and material artefact for the facilitation of critical, creative and consilient thinking and teaching about controversial issues.

Marilyn Ahearn
is an adjunct lecturer at SCU. She has extensive experience in primary education, including participation and leadership in environmental education initiatives. Marilyn completed her PhD at SCU and continues to collaborate in writing projects as a member of the 'Sustainability, Environment, the Arts in Education' (SEAE) Research Cluster. She is committed to researching and promoting a universal deep-time story through environmental education and transdisciplinary-based learning in the primary school setting.

William Boyd
is a professor and member of the Emeritus Faculty at Southern Cross University. He is a multi- and trans-disciplinary scholar, geographer, social scientist and educationalist. His interests span environmental change, social dimensions of environment, and education, particularly concerning the social construction of environment, educational futures, and the scholarship of teaching & learning. His current scholarly focusses is on exploring innovative cultural approaches to scholarship and the processes of scholarly inquiry.

Euan Boyd
is an emerging visual artist and illustrator who is currently undertaking a Bachelor of Creative Industries at the Queensland University of Technology.

Euan's visual arts practice is concerned with exploring ideas of sustainability within creative and illustrative art practice. Euan does so by investigating representations of ecological monstrosities by utilising repurposed and recycled found materiality and integrating new and emerging digital technologies.

Adrienne Brown
is a practicing Visual Artist and Senior Lecturer in Creative Technologies at Hunan City University, and Hangzhou Vocational and Technical College, China for Whitireia Polytech, Aotearoa. Adi's experience spans over 20 years of lecturing, curating and art making. Her MFA thesis explored notions of the feminist uncanny, photography and object making and currently she is concerned with walking and drawing in place as a response to climate change. Adi has published and exhibited widely internationally and in Aotearoa and her work was included in a national survey show at Pataka Gallery, Wellington and The Sargent Gallery, Whanganui. She has been a finalist in a range of national art awards, including Aotearoa's prestigious annual Wallace Art Awards. Adi moved to Queensland to be with her partner in 2017, where they live with their beloved animal family. She is currently a PhD candidate and member of the Sustainability, Environment, and the Arts in Education (SEAE) Research Cluster at Southern Cross University, Australia. Adi is committed to arts-based education that is collaborative and project based, and her research interests are in Visual Arts pedagogies in higher education.

Shae Brown
is an educator with extensive experience with in a wide range of learning environments. Currently Shae is undertaking a Doctoral research project at Southern Cross University, Australia. Shae is passionate about the knowledges required by all young people today to face the challenges of the C21. Drawing on her practice with secondary students, Shae's project contributes a patterns-based approach to the teaching and learning of complexity competence. It is a strategy and process for enabling embodied knowledge of/as/with complex phenomena, using pattern thinking as an accessible language for all students. Through diffractive relationality of Indigenous Knowledge and the quantum field theory of agential realism, Shae's project contributes to the understanding of the co-generative relationality of the human and more-then-human world in both complex phenomena and knowledge production. Shae is also the Senior Student Advocate at Southern Cross University and actively represents postgraduate students as President of the Southern Cross Postgraduate Association and as a Member of the National Council of Australian Postgraduate Associations.

Teresa Carapeto
is a teacher in Steiner education and a PhD student at SCU. She earned a scholarship to complete her PhD in exploring Steiner education and its conceptions of nature in the context of environmental education research. Teresa earned an Australian College of Educator's World Teacher's Day award for outstanding graduate in 2017. She was awarded a scholarship to complete her honours research in 'embedding environmental education in the history classroom'. Teresa gained a scholarship to travel to India to research the Ancient Hindu Empire. In 2015, she was awarded a scholarship to travel to Barcelona to complete an Independent Research Project focused on artist Gaudi. Teresa is committed to drawing on her research to contribute to global environmental education research, by way of publications and presentations on the insights of Steiner education. She has published collaboratively with colleagues from the Sustainability, Environment and the Arts in Education Research Cluster (SEAE).

Philemon Chigeza
is a senior lecturer at James Cook University. He is an experienced mathematics teacher and lecturer with a research interest in the ethnomathematics of representation in physical, blended and virtual learning spaces. Philemon's earlier research focused on developing capacity building pedagogies that affirm students' lived languages, experiences and knowledge in their learning. His work explores the notion of agency and students' negotiation of language and culture in mathematics and science classrooms. Much of his present research is focused on emerging technology-based curriculum innovation designed to enhance engagement and learning, particularly for blended and virtual spaces. Philemon is also passionate about issues of environmental sustainability and how schools, electronic media and the home can be productively used to work towards a more sustainable and just society.

Amy Cutter-Mackenzie-Knowles
is a Professor of Sustainability, Environment and Education at Southern Cross University. She is the Executive Dean of the Faculty of Education, as well as the Research Leader of the 'Sustainability, Environment and the Arts in Education' (SEAE) Research Cluster. Amy's research centres on climate change, childhood-nature, posthuman philosophy, and child-framed research methodologies. She is particularly focussed on the pivot points between environmental education, science, philosophy, and the Arts. Amy has been recognised for both her teaching and research excellence in environmental education, including the Australian Association for Environmental Education Fellowship (Life Achievement Award) for her outstanding contribution to environmental education research.

David Ellis
is a former high school technology teacher, head teacher and VET coordinator who has worked across both New South Wales State and Catholic Education systems, and consulted in technology curriculum development. During his time in schools, he experienced the challenges that teachers face alone, in leadership and in management, in an effort to maintain their expertise in an evolving educational landscape. As a consequence, his research interests took a turn towards an important, and ongoing issue in education – teacher expertise and professional learning. This formed the basis of his PhD research. Dave has continued to published in books and journals a number of areas, such as interdisciplinary education projects, project-based learning, communities of practice and has an interest in the transformative learning processes that occur through collaboration and experiential learning.

Katie Hotko
is an Associate Lecturer in the Faculty of Education at Southern Cross University, where she is also an active member of the Sustainability, Environment and the Arts in Education (SEAE) Research Cluster. Katie's is in the final stages of her PhD exploring Primary Teachers' self-beliefs about creativity, and how these beliefs effect their teaching of the Visual Arts. Katie is a self-taught artist who is passionate about making the Visual Arts accessible to all people. Through the lens of process philosophy and a/r/tography, her inquiry delves into the becoming of the creative self-identities of practicing generalist primary teachers in the Visual Arts.

Rita L. Irwin
is a Distinguished University Scholar and Professor of Art Education and Curriculum Studies, former Associate Dean of Teacher Education, and former Head of the Department of Curriculum Studies at The University of British Columbia, Vancouver, BC, Canada. She has been an educational leader for a number of provincial, national and international organizations, including being President of the Canadian Society for the Study of Education, Canadian Association of Curriculum Studies, Canadian Society for Education through Art, International Society for Education through Art and Chair of the World Alliance for Arts Education. Her research interests have spanned in-service art education, teacher education, socio-cultural issues, and curriculum practices across K-12 and informal learning settings. She publishes widely, exhibits her artworks, and has secured a range of research grants allowing her to work internationally. She is best known for her work in a/r/tography that expands collaborative arts collectives. She is very proud of how collected works and edited volumes have been translated into nearly a dozen languages.

Ferdousi Khatun

is an independent scholar and completed her PhD in the School of Education, at Southern Cross University. Ferdousi is passionate about Environmental Education. She is a member of the Sustainability, Environment and the Arts in Education Research Cluster. Her PhD focussed on Bangladeshi young people's ecoliteracy, applying a postcolonial socioecological theoretical framework. In addition to undertaking her PhD, Ferdousi worked as a research assistant and casual academic in the School of Education, Southern Cross University. She has extensive experience as a teacher, environmental educator and botanist in Bangladesh, Nepal and Australia.

Alexandra Lasczik

is Professor, Arts & Education in the Faculty of Education at Southern Cross University, Australia. She is currently Associate Dean Research in the Faculty of Education, and Research co-Leader of the Sustainability, Environment and the Arts in Education (SEAE) Research Cluster. Lexi is an expert educator with almost 40 years experience in the Visual Arts. She is also a practicing artist whose chosen mediums are painting, photography, poetry, walking and creative writing. Travel, movement and migrations are large themes in Lexi's work, as are the Arts and Arts-based Educational Research (ABER), particularly A/r/tography. Lexi is an *Artivist*, committed to equity and social justice, and her spirited advocacy of a high quality Arts education for all spans across her entire career. Lexi brings extensive teaching experience in the Arts in Australia and internationally and is a specialist with respect to the Visual Arts, teaching and learning, creative curriculum design and innovative pedagogies, with particular expertise in the engagement of at-risk youth through the Arts. Lexi brings this extensive experience and depth of understanding of the sector to her influential work in teacher education at Southern Cross University.

Marianne Logan

is a researcher and lecturer at Southern Cross University in Science and Technology education. She is a founding executive member of the Sustainability, Environment and the Arts in Education (SEAE) Research Cluster. Marianne's teaching/learning is a central focus in her research endeavours and this is further supported by her commitment and contribution to the education profession particularly in the areas of science and sustainability. She is passionate about inspiring learners to become aware of environmental sustainability and providing platforms for their voices to be heard. Marianne's recent research involves child/youth framed, arts based, research and she is coordinating several research projects including projects that have received external funding. Marianne collaborates closely with community members and environmental organisations in school projects and collaborative grants to inform and facilitate environmental education in the community. The findings from Marianne's research have been presented at international and national conferences and published in International research journals and edited texts. Marianne has co-supervised Honours and PhD candidates through to completion and is currently supervising Honours, PhD and EdD candidates.

Alys Mendus
is originally from the UK. She is an Independent Scholar and Casual Academic at University of Melbourne, Victoria and at Southern Cross University (online), currently based just north of Brisbane, QLD, Australia. She is fascinated by 'things' that have agency to impact upon our lives and exploring this dynamic intra-play between the human/non-human. In 2018 she invited members of the public to 'Come Dance My PhD' which was made into a film and a reflexive epilogue recently, published in Murmurations journal. Her autoethnographic PhD embodied her rhizomatic nomadology, living as a van-dweller, constantly travelling, writing in/into changing environments as she was performing School Tourism: Searching for the Ideal School around the World. She did not find the Ideal School but she did fall in love, moved to the other side of the world and recently had her first child. Alys is a key member of the Bodies Collective, a group of international Early Career Researchers seeking to challenge and change hegemonic forms of research that privilege mind over body.

Yaw Ofosu-Asare
is a PhD candidate at Southern Cross University-Australia. He is a leading thinker on indigenous graphical representations, and the role lived-experience can play in the equitable development of transformative design education curriculum. With over ten years of experience co-developing multi-sector innovation strategies and shaping policy with global institutions, his research focuses on indigenous pedagogy and transformative systems across education, design and manufacturing industries. Currently, Yaw is researching novel design-driven processes engaging indigenous knowledge systems in developing curriculum resource of design education. Yaw obtained a BA Graphic design at University of Education, Winneba and MPhil in Art Education at Kwame Nkrumah University of Science and Technology, Ghana.

Maia Osborn
is a Research Fellow with the Sustainability, Environment and the Arts in Education Research Cluster within the School of Education at Southern Cross University on the Gold Coast. Maia's research interests include posthumanism,

social ecology, holistic environmental education, climate change education, community partnerships, experiential pedagogies, nature play and STEM. Maia's PhD research explored environmentally conscious teachers' philosophies, pedagogies, practices, and the value of community partnerships to enrich environmental education.

Marie-Laurence Paquette
is a PhD candidate at Southern Cross University, Australia. After completing her bachelor of Environmental Geography (UdeM, Canada) and master's in Use and Conservation of Natural Resources with a focus on coastal oceanography (UFSC, Brazil), she redirected her focus from academic research to community engagement with a desire to bring Earth sciences knowledge closer to communities. Since 2016, Mahi does so by working closely with/for notfor-profit organisations, coordinating teams, campaigns and events with educational purposes. Her current projects, professional and academic, are designed to expand the scope of understanding of social changes associated with planetary conditions and the Earth system as a whole, including human wellbeing. Mahi is passionate about addressing humanity's challenges ahead, especially the ones associated with threats to the life support system such as biodiversity loss, climate change, wealth inequalities, pollution and oceanic changes. Her thesis looks at understanding and mapping the transition between the current paradigm of business as usual in SMEs and the next paradigm, using theories of poststructuralism, postmodernism and posthumanism as bridging inquiries through methodologies associated with pedagogy of wisdom and experience learning.

Jemma Peisker
is an Associate Lecturer and the Course Coordinator for the Doctor of Education and Bachelor of Education (Honours) programs in the Faculty of Education at Southern Cross University, Australia. Jemma has a Graduate Diploma in Education, a Bachelor of Fine Art, Honours in Fine Arts, Bachelor of Education Honours (First Class), and Doctor of Philosophy. For her Honours work, Jemma was awarded the Southern Cross University Medal for Research in 2015, and received the Australian Postgraduate Award for her Doctoral Studies in 2016. Jemma was also awarded the Higher Degrees Research Excellence Award in 2018. Jemma's research uses ABER methodologies, and has a focus on the primacy of material engagement in Environmental and Arts Education. She explores the way bodily activity, cultural practices, learning settings and transformations in material culture can positively affect students psycho-cally and how this may influence students' schooling and learning exper

Ziah Peisker
is a middle-school student in South East Queensland. In this publication, he co-authored a chapter on risky socio-ecological learning; fittingly Ziah is an active young person. At fourteen years old, Ziah takes physical 'risks' in his daily life as he applies discipline in his sporting endeavours and physical activities. He is a 1st Dan Blackbelt in Tae Kwon Do, a silver and bronze medallist at the 2021 Queensland State Surf Life Saving Championships, a district pool swimming representative, and a keen sprinter and archer. He also enjoys riding, ocean swimming, and camping. In 2020 Ziah was selected by his school to have his work self-published in an anthology of short stories. Ziah is a dedicated student who excels in science and maths subjects, and hopes to study medicine or science at university when he graduates school.

Adrienne Piscopo
is an emerging visual artist and researcher who utilises an interdisciplinary approach to Arts Based Research and studio practice. Adrienne has just completed her Bachelor of Fine Arts (Honours) at the Queensland College of Art, Griffith, and has a Bachelor of Fine Arts (Visual Arts) from the Queensland University of Technology. Her visual art practice is often focused on exploring the notion of liminal space through representations of voids, circular shapes, and centralised open aperture forms.

David Rousell
is a Senior Lecturer in Creative Education at RMIT University, where he is a core member of the Creative Agency Lab. Prior to joining RMIT David was Senior Lecturer at Manchester Metropolitan University, where he coordinated the Manifold Lab for Biosocial Studies in the Education and Social Research Institute. David's research combines his work in affect studies, digital ethnography, and posthumanism with his professional background as an environmental artist, designer, and arts educator. He is invested in the ecological rethinking of the politics and ethics of digital life through critical and creative engagements with sensory technologies and media.

Ben Ryan
is an established Principal at Monkland State School, near Gympie and above Queensland's Sunshine Coast. Ben has a Bachelor of Education, a Graduate Certificate in Training & Development and a Masters in Learning & Development, Educational Leadership. Ben is an active student of the outdoors and all the learning available through its offerings – Ben has qualifications and interests in rock-climbing and abseiling, bushwalking and trail running,

archery and most water sports. Ben is an advocate for Outdoor Education and outdoor learning opportunities in schools to enrich engagement and self-efficacy in learning and development.

Billy Ryan
is a middle-school student in Gympie, above Queensland's Sunshine Coast. In this publication, he contributed to a chapter on risky socio-ecological learning; drawing upon his active outdoor lifestyle. At fourteen, Billy is a positive risk taker, an accomplished athlete and an inspired student of math, science and English. Billy is a multiple participant of Queensland Cross-Country Championships and the winner of various long-distance races around Queensland. Billy holds a 4th Dan grey belt in Brazilian Jiu-Jitsu, and is an active archer, rock-climber and paddler. He enjoys reading and camping as a passive interest. Billy hopes to work outdoors in an Environmental Science or Engineering field in his future.

Lisa Siegel
is an Associate Lecturer in the Faculty of Education at Southern Cross University, where she is also an active member of the Sustainability, Environment and the Arts in Education (SEAE) Research Cluster. Lisa is currently completing her PhD research which focuses on the collective stories of the lived experiences of women environmentalists. Lisa has been an environmental educator in her regional Australian community for fifteen years, having founded the not for profit Centre for Ecological Learning in Bellingen, NSW, which provides nature connection education for all ages. She also co-convenes the Mid North Coast Sustainability Education Network (AAEE-NSW).

Helen Widdop Quinton
is a Lecturer in the College of Arts & Education and a Research Fellow with the Institute of Sustainable Industries and Liveable Cities at Victoria University, Melbourne. She works with situated knowledge, with a particular focus on socioecological learning through place-attuned and relational pedagogies for sustaining the wellbeing of people, places and planetary systems. Recently her research has been geared towards identifying conceptual tools for stimulating a perspective shift to an interconnected planetary health worldview.

Thilinika Wijesinghe
is a PhD candidate at Southern Cross University. She is an active member of the Sustainability, Environment and the Arts in Education (SEAE) Research Cluster. Her PhD study explores how children and young people may be able

to express their worldviews on climate change through a relatively new method called Speculative Drama. Thilinika also works as a Research Assistant in the School of Education at Southern Cross University. Her interests are in childhood research, environmental education, climate change education, creative and critical thinking, art-based research, drama-based research and digital pedagogies. Thilinika's childhood experiences growing up in rural Sri Lanka, strongly influence her values, interests, research and practice.

Tracy Young
is a lecturer and researcher from Swinburne University, Melbourne. Tracy's research adopts postqualitative methodologies that invite creative practices for generating conceptual understandings while theorising with critical posthumanist, ecofeminist and new materialist philosophies. Tracy engages with human-animal studies where the complex relations with children, animals and environments provide a space for ethical inquiry that troubles how animal species are socially constructed, culturally reproduced and positioned in early childhood education. Tracy's research contributes to wider understandings about the significance of early childhood education in terms of relationality with the human and the more-than-human.

PROLOGUE

Fold, Unfolding, Enfolding

Socioecological Learning through Arts-Based Thought Experiments

Alexandra Lasczik and Amy Cutter-Mackenzie-Knowles

The Sustainability, Environment and the Arts in Education (SEAE) Research Cluster[1] in the Faculty of Education at Southern Cross University, Australia, is a collective of Environmental and Arts educators who seek to enact profound change in/through transdisciplinary environmental and Arts education research that disrupts and generates new ways of being and becoming. We are a close-knit and textured group of dedicated senior academics, early- and mid-career researchers and doctoral students who seek to engage in creative research practices to disrupt and transform ecological thought and action in the context of anthropogenic climate change.

In doing this, we have focused in the past years on bringing our members together in-place on Bundjalung Country for a series of highly productive writing retreats, where our researchers work towards assembling projects and collections of global and local significance, engaging in transformational research in Environmental and Arts education that 'matters'. In this past 'COVID year', it has not been possible to gather in-place, yet we have continued our work remotely, until it has been possible to gather together once more. Indeed, we write this prologue at our first 'live' retreat in a long while, some two years after we began working on this book and just as we are about to go to press – a collection that had its genesis in the same location as we are in now.

There is something very powerful in the initiative of in-place collectivity, stripped from the demands of everyday academic life. Dynamisms and concepts are able to gestate and form; we have the time to slow down and engage in the deep intellectual work that the academy demands, yet often precludes (Lasczik Cutcher & Irwin, 2017). Writing on retreat also engages a "collective feminist ethics of care" – indeed, such slow scholarship is committed to collective and communal high-quality research, that proponents argue is a radical necessity (Mountz, et al., 2015, p. 2). The writing retreat affords us all the opportunity to "stretch time, to prolong experience, to deeply and gently engage with our wonderings and wanderings, experimentally" (Lasczik Cutcher & Irwin, 2017, p. 2) and its engagement in SEAE affords possibility and productivity for our members. In our workings as the leaders of SEAE

 | DOI:10.1163/9789004507838_001

(Cutter-Mackenzie-Knowles & Lasczik), we also seek to do more than simply make space for scholarship and slow down. We also seek to deeply enact our responsibilities as senior academics, to 'send the elevator back down' for our colleagues who might need it, through mentoring and career support, whilst also looking outwards together towards our national and international connections and folding them into our SEAE activities.

The resonances we are experiencing today as we write and experience the site of this retreat again, shatter though our memories and collide with the next project we have under development. We fold the previous experiences of creating collections through the collegial scholarship of SEAE into the new folds of future work, creasing and pleating and gathering anew, as we have done previously, with this collection and others. Indeed, this book draws from a previous work also conceptualised on retreat, one which is deeply theoretically layered and intensely philosophical. This new work diffracts from the reference work into a completely new creation, one which is both connected to and transcendent from the original scholarship that gives it its breath.

This new work therefore seeks to be an arts-based companion – but also a standalone book – to our previous title *Touchstones for Deterritorializing Socioecological Learning – The Anthropocene, Posthumanism and Common Worlds as Creative Milieux* (Cutter-Mackenzie-Knowles et al., 2020).[2] This new offering both folds into and unfolds away from *Touchstones,* drawing from each chapter in turn, experimenting with thought, engaging Arts forms, practices and praxes in order to work the concepts and positionings, pushing them outwards through diffractions and sustained investigations. This new work is highly original and distinctive through its focus on the socioecological learner through arts-based experimentations. In the era of the Anthropocene, thinking of learning in socioecological terms is paramount – and thinking through the forms of the arts offers a fresh and original proposition.

Touchstones is a complex and highly theoretical offering to the field of education and particularly to socioecological learning. We offer *Arts-Based Thought Experiments* as a creative compendium that complements, experiments with and portrays the complexities and praxes of the original book, through the engagement of arts-based forms and methods in order to offer an analysis that unpacks the original work for a broader audience than the merely academic (Brown & Fehige, 2014; Pente, 2018). It seeks to be a more accessible title, a more artfully positioned one that engages visual arts, photography, poetry, creative non-fiction, memoir and fiction. As such it contributes to the fields of education, environmental education, Arts education, educational research and arts-based educational research in myriad and useful ways. Yet, this work goes further, and beyond our original imaginings of socioecological learning into new territories. In this new book, we lean far more deeply into concepts of the imaginary, troubling the tensions between the human and the posthuman.

Arts-Based Thought Experiments is a highly visual offering, poetic and aesthetic, with some of the authors from *Touchstones* included together with new authors engaging new concepts, practices and processes. We have drawn significantly from the methodologies of Arts-based research in this work, which transcend qualitative inquiry in convention and practice (Knight & Lasczik Cutcher, 2018; Springgay et al., 2005). Arts-based research is its own modality, defying traditional conventions of methodology and inquiry. It does so in order to seek to engage in living inquiry through the practices and processes of making artworks as data creation and analytical flourish, entwining and weaving inter- and intra-textualities of the poetic and prosaic with the visual and performative. These aesthetic entanglings create, through the architectures of engagement, a suite of deeply aesthetic experiences for the reader in simulacra – in this case – of place.

At our writing retreat in 2019, we began through play, to experiment and push and fold and stretch the *Touchstones* concepts of the Anthropocene, posthumanism and common worlds as creative milieux, through new diffractions and new site-specific experimentations, many of which are shared in this volume. This opened up spaces for deep relatings with/as the Earth since place was foregrounded in our scholarship. We walked the site of the grand house in which we dwelled for the 3 days, with its magnificent grounds – once paddocks, now reclaimed rainforest – stumbling upon hidden messages and corners, making artworks and poetry, performances and experiences, creating and collecting data through the events of the retreat. We took away with us, folded into our collective memory, the experiences of the retreat and its documented forms, to craft the chapters and artworks as author groups, reconnecting from time to time throughout that first COVID year. We were stalled in our writing, and then stalled again in the review process, as we and our colleagues were entrenched in the labour of working, teaching and writing remotely in pandemic times. Similarly, our precious reviewers were delayed for the same reasons. Yet these chapters also sustained us, and we turned to the creative satisfaction of crafting new work again and again until we were done.

Underneath the layers of thought, of experimentation and crafting, is the collective experience and collective memory of the place of the retreat, the beautiful Diptipur in northern New South Wales, Australia. Its presence shatters and resonates throughout the chapters, so that the reader may experience the traces of this place, and our experiences here. In our folding, unfolding and enfolding of concepts, we have engaged in the creation of the new: new thinkings, new doings and new tellings for deep relatings with/as the Earth.

Diptipur (on Bundjalung Country), April 2021

Notes

1 You can find more information here: https://www.scu.edu.au/education/research/sustainability-environment-and-the-arts-in-education-seae-research-cluster/
2 It can be found here: https://www.palgrave.com/gp/book/9783030122119

References

Brown, J. R., & Fehige, Y. (2014). Thought experiments. In E. N. Zalta (Ed.), *Stanford encyclopedia of philosophy*. http://plato.stanford.edu/archives/fall2014/entries/thought-experiment/

Cutter-Mackenzie-Knowles, A., Lasczik, A., Wilks, J., Logan, M., Turner, A., & Boyd, W. (2020). *Touchstones for deterritorialising socioecological learning: The Anthropocene, posthumanism and common worlds as creative milieux*. Palgrave Macmillan.

Knight, L., & Lasczik Cutcher, A. (Eds.). (2018). *Arts-research-education: Connections and directions*. Springer.

Lasczik Cutcher, A., & Irwin, R. L. (2017). Walkings-through paint: A c/a/r/tography of slow scholarship. *Journal of Curriculum and Pedagogy, 14*(2). doi:10.1080/15505170.2017.1310680

Mountz, A., Bonds, A., Mansfield, B., Loyd, J., Hyndman, J., & Walton-Roberts, M. (2015). For slow scholarship: A feminist politics of resistance through collective action in the neoliberal university. *ACME: An International EJournal. for Critical Geographies, 14*(4), 1235–1259.

Pente, P. V. (2018). Posthumanism and arts-based educational research exploration in 3D and 4D digital fabrication. In L. Knight & A. Lasczik Cutcher (Eds.), *Arts-research-education* (pp. 135–149). Springer.

Springgay, S., Irwin, R. L., & Kind, S. W. (2005). A/r/tography as living inquiry through art and text. *Qualitative Inquiry, 11*(6), 897–912.

CHAPTER 1

Who Can Speak for the Earth?

Working the Socioecological Touchstones of the Anthropocene, the Posthuman and Common Worlds through the Creative Milieux of Speculative Fiction

Alexandra Lasczik and Amy Cutter-Mackenzie-Knowles

Abstract

This chapter seeks to activate (through arts-based methods), socioecological learning, which was introduced in the original chapter, entitled "Touchstones for Deterritorializing the Socioecological Learner" (Cutter-Mackenzie-Knowles et al., 2020). The Touchstones are the Anthropocene, the Posthuman and Common Worlds as Creative Milieux. This assemblage opens up the space for de-learning and de-imagining[1] the learner as a socioecological learner. This chapter has thus been written as speculative fiction, because we wanted to provoke further accessible dialogue around these deeply theoretical constructs.

We worked through a process similar to that of the Surrealist invention of 'le cadaver exquis' (exquisite corpse). This was a parlour game of drawing, whereby the artists take turns to create an image with guidelines or prompts, not viewing what the artist before them had created, the result of which was a Surrealist drawing. The reason we did this was that we sought an enigmatic conversation, a playful exchange, in keeping with notions of engaged and pleasurable learning experiences. Thus, we handed the manuscript backwards and forwards to each other in a socioecological dialogue, working the Touchstones in practice.

The aim of the writing-as-inquiry (Richardson, 2003) was to create, to generate, to explore, to provoke. We asserted our own guidelines and prompts, engaging enabling constraints after Manning and Massumi (2014) in order to create in a more focused way, allowing our creativity its breath. We therefore constrained the word limit for each pass: 250–500 words, with a 24-hour turnaround. Whilst we did not always strictly adhere to the constraints, what we found was that such a dialogue can take the writer to unexpected places, and that we were entirely engaged in the project, often eschewing other more pressing work to linger in the act of writing.

We also found that we were eager to trouble the tensions around anthropomorphising more than human entities, given that, as humans, we know no other onto-epistemological perspective than that of our own. As we wrote ourselves into the more than

 | DOI:10.1163/9789004507838_002

human characters, we pondered that the learner in the context of education is ineffably human, as are we, the authors. We can no more speak as a dolphin or a spider than the spider or dolphin can speak for us. We can however, imagine, create, and speculate as socioecological learners. Indeed, we cannot speak for the Earth, although when attempted to connect, we found that the Earth likely had a lot to say.

Keywords

carbon – COVID-19 – matter – thought experiment – arts-based STEM – story

Matter Matters

I looked down on Abigail as she lay dying, thinking about her imminent transmogrification and the events of the next hours and days. She'd be dead by midnight, two hours away.

There is nobody here with her, just me. I hover here, contemplating this rude disruption to her otherwise healthy existence. Her death is somewhat senseless, but an object lesson in these days, and I contributed to it, ultimately.

Her breath is becoming ever so laboured now, the ventilator has been removed, offering her some final peace. The doctors thought she would rally; she seemed to be doing so well. In their medical arrogance they failed to see what I can. Life is temporary and fleeting, and all life ends. Humans think their lives as they know it will go on forever, and thus they do everything they can to extend it – as if they are the centre of the universe and in control of it all.

What humans stupidly fail to understand in their arrogance is that they are but one species, but one cohort of sentient beings. That's it, that's all. They are *one*.

They think they are the only beings with a capacity for reason, a trait that can sometimes be their downfall. They cling to impermanent things, not realising that nothing is permanent. They are incapable of authentic satisfaction, always craving pleasure, craving more. What humans often do not acknowledge, is that life for all on this planet is painful, impermanent and in constant movement and flux. Death is the only thing that is real, true and predetermined. The only thing they can rely upon really.

Abigail is perhaps just realising this now, as she loiters on the doorstep of her own death. Her eyes flutter and her hands drum her chest, reflexive energy leaving her body, trickling away. Her breath is getting laboured and slower; it won't be long now.

I bend close to her ear, stroke her hair, and say, "Go calmly Abigail, this is not the end. You will always remain with me". She cannot hear me, but it needs to be said. This is how this part ends for every being. You can only die by yourself.

As I linger beside her, I want to tell her, but she will find out herself soon enough. Her life is not ending, she is merely becoming something else. She will never fully disappear. Traces will always remain.

I know this because what she will become is more of me. I know what you're thinking, but you're likely wrong.

I'm not the Divine – not God, Allah, the Great Spirit or the Rainbow Serpent. I'm not any of those transcendental things, but rather something far more concrete.

I am simply **Matter**, and I am in all things.

A Glass of CHNOPS

Well, yes you are in all things Matter because you are indeed every *thing*. It seems like everyone is talking about you these days, ever since Barad's[2] "Meeting the Universe Halfway" became the latest philosophical freak show. She says that matter and meaning are inseparable. She is right of course, but what I quite like about you Matter, is time and what you do with it. You just keep metamorphising into something else, or nothing at all. But of course, it's never just nothing.

Those humans talk about me sometimes too, but not much. They most often don't think about me, except for the scientists or the scientifically aware. Perhaps the philosophers at times. Maybe students when they have to … but the others, not at all. This is likely because I exist beyond the acknowledgement or consciousness of most.

I am **CHNOPS** – the six most *important* elements of life. I say this unashamedly because without me, there would be nothing but the inert. I am carbon, hydrogen, nitrogen, oxygen, phosphorus, and sulfur. I am in 99% of all life. Actually, I am life. You just take up space Matter, but I am the stuff that gives you agency; that makes you matter, Matter.

Your beloved Abigail could simply not have existed without me. She was quite the character though, wasn't she, our Abigail? Always fighting for a post-carbon future, as if that was ever going to happen. I mean, WTF!? There is no such thing as *post*-carbon – it's in everything! How amusing it is that Abigail did not know that she herself was actually 18% carbon.

That carbon is only one of my vital elements, but it sure gets a bad rap. I cannot operate without carbon. Carbon is the king of the elements; it's the bee's knees, the cat's meow. My carbon-bonds is where the magic is. Oh, how

I love my carbon-bonds! Carbon-bonds are what makes me a *chain-gang* – literally sticking my elements together like white on rice. I would be nowhere without them!

Bonds aside, what needs to be understood is that life would be *impossible* without carbon. So, for goodness' sake, would you humans stop all this nonsense about a post-carbon future? It is an impossible reality, and your ignorance is becoming nauseating.

The problem actually is that humans like my carbon too much – way too much. I know carbon is gorgeous; look at diamonds, graphite, coal, oil! Pretty, useful and compelling. Shall I go on? For example, when something dies (like Abigail), I turn much of it into carbon (yes Matter, I know, that's you too). And the carbon never really disappears. It just keeps cycling around like night and day. The problem is that those humans go to great lengths to find it, dig it up, burn it, release it. They just cannot leave it alone, prone to excess as they are. Well, I need to put that carbon somewhere, and as Matter rightly says, it cannot disappear, it just transmogrifies. So, as a result there are now 411.15 ppm (parts per million) of carbon dioxide (CO_2) in the atmosphere and it is not my fault – it has to go somewhere! Only 100 years ago it was 300 ppm. And 40,000 years ago, it was 200 ppm. You do the maths. This is the fault of the humans, they did this, so don't look at me. All I'll say is that I hope you like it hot!

Rondure

Thanks, CHNOPS and Matter; I'll take it from here. You are indeed both vital to life and to all things – from the organic to the inorganic, the sentient and those that are not-conscious-of-being-conscious.

I think that covers everyone.

Matter thinks that they are omnipotent and CHNOPS is just a bruiser who likes to push folks around. The arrogance of them both! It is so unbecoming … Still, it is an arrogance borne of quantum reality, so I'll let it go for now because they transcend me, into our universe and beyond through time and space. For me, they are everything, and I simply would not exist without them – because I too, am unique. But we are entwined, an assemblage of all things to have ever existed; we are companions, allies, associates. An ecology of life in its most fundamental form.

I am the only terrene in my sister's domain – the universe – that holds life on its surfaces; a blue marble, an astronomical object, the third rock from the sun. I am 4.5 billion years young, in an intimate relationship with my moon and the sun, tilting and spinning and changing my surface tectonically over millions of years. The gravitational pull from my only satellite, my beloved moon, stabilises me, slows me down and determines the tidal flows of the water on my surface – all two-thirds of it – my hydrosphere. My core is solidly iron, surrounded by liquid magnetics, my mantle, tectonic plates, crust and a third of my surface, land. I am Gaia, Gaea, Terra, Tellus, Planet: of course, **I am the Earth**.

From my perspective, it is essential to understand that I (Earth) am not the same thing as the *world*. I am entity, object, terrain, planet. World is an ineffably human idea because it refers to the part of me that humans can access with their minds and bodies, and all other beings on me. It has to do with my surface, all life and human hierarchies. The concept of world is an entirely human concept, an abstract, a metaphor, a psychological construct, a philosophical domain. It includes life, the universe and everything but also language and emotions. For example, humans might say, "I want to see the world", meaning they want to travel to places. Or they say, "You are my whole world", to their beloved, meaning they are above all others in their heart. And sometimes they refer to, "It's a world-wide phenomenon", usually meaning something to do with human behaviour or effects. They also allude to inner 'worlds' or sub-worlds – like the 'world' of work, or the 'world' of fashion. 'Common worlds' mean places occupied by many. It is a complex construct for sure, but one that is entirely the province of the human.

World*ing* is far more interesting to me. New materialists like Kathleen Stewart[3] speak of the affective nature and agency of all non-human beings, and their entanglements. This is something I have always known, that all matter, all CHNOPs, all ecologies, all beings – every*thing* – are equal and in ecology with all others.

But I'm getting ahead of myself. Before I look at ontologies, it is important that I explore the impact of the human on me. Because that is the most pressing issue of this moment, at least for the humans.

We Are All Made of Dinosaur Pee

It's time for me to weigh back in here Earth, being CHNOPS and all. Y'all need to listen to me because I'm important.

While I don't consciously create any life, watching and participating in the evolution of the human has been an interesting blip in time. Probably not as interesting as the dinosaurs though … gee, that was a scary 165 million years! It got loud, real loud! Love me some dinosaur, and I miss them, but they're still with us. It's like when that human dude Collin Mochrie, you know that funny guy, said, "we all have a dinosaur deep within us just trying to get out".

We sure do have dinosaurs deep within – everything on Earth still has dinosaur smatterings – wee, shite, all of it really in just about everything! The traces remain, as you said Earth.

I do remember when it all began 4.5 billion years ago – at least for you Earth! CHNOPS gets around – you're not my first planet, you know. It's been bumpy – all of these changes. Yeah, yeah, I know I've been at the centre of a few epochal changes. Like this latest one – the Anthropocene/Capitalocene/Plantationocene/Chthulucene – or whatever it's called … I don't care much what it is called, but it is the sixth extinction event on you Earth and it's keeping me real busy.

Humans have caused the Anthropocene. They are the Anthropocene. Anthropocene literally means the epoch of the human. That Italian chick – what's her name? Braidotti?[4] – anyway she said that it's the *biogentic age* because humans have the power to disrupt the ecological balance – and they have with their endless wastefulness and attachment to fossil fuels, technology and science. And it's not just the carbon or 'climate change' as they call it. Those humans just make more and more and more and more *stuff* – or more matter as you would say Matter. And more and more humans are making more and more stuff. They're a trip! There is no place on you Earth now, that humans have not infiltrated, no untouched wild ecosystems anymore. They are everywhere. They've even changed the chemical composition of the atmosphere – now that takes some doing. It's like they want to extinguish their own selves.

And now, can you believe it Matter, those mod-con humans think they're cyborgs. Too many Terminator movies, you ask me. Like humans could ever do what I do naturally, with their low-grade tech. Just digging a bigger hole for themselves really. More matter, hey Matter!

What humans don't get is that it makes no difference to me what they are. They are mostly microbiota anyway – just like every other living thing as Abigail understands now, I'm sure. Their bits might go on and turn into something else too. Just like the dinos!

"Given enough time, everything becomes digestable to bacteria", said Hird and Yusoff[5] and they really nailed it there! Everything can and will be consumed by bacteria – and that's what is important to me – life!

Humans are no more important to me than any other species, although I reckon the echidnas are the coolest. They're so smart! Smarter than humans by far. Their prefrontal cortex is bigger than any other mammal.[6] You know, I did that. That stuff is all me. But hey, size isn't everything, even though echidnas are wise, and smart as a whip. They do some of the most complex thinking of anyone on Earth. They've been around a while too – about 50 million years. Modern humans have only been around 200,000 years. Oh, they're so much work, I so prefer their ancestors. I bet you do too, hey Earth!

The Land Will Move You

I prefer them too; yes, I agree with you CHNOPS. They were so much smarter. If life in ancient times was so simple as modern humans seem to think, how did humans develop their large brain? And why can't they use more of it? This is just another example of human ignorance – and there are *so many* examples. They don't even realise that their brain capacity was developed in land-based cultures – that's right. Place. Me. Engagement with me. As that bloke Tyson says, "*if you don't move with the land, the land will move you*. There is nothing permanent about settlements and the civilisations that spawn them".[7]

And that is what is happening now. The land (me) will move humans on, because they are doing so much damage, and they will see, just as I have seen, that their civilisations will end – like the Mayans, the Egyptians, the Sumerians, the Romans … I am heating up rapidly and it's becoming very uncomfortable (thanks CHNOPS). My creatures are dying and disappearing forever, and this is mostly the fault of arrogant, over consuming, humans. There are simply too many of them, and they are impacting me in ways I've never experienced before. Sure, I've been hit by asteroids and supervolcanoes, had major tectonic shifts, been exposed to cosmic radiation and ice ages … but this? This isn't nature taking its course, its humans causing the excess of carbon in the atmosphere, ocean acidity, flora and fauna disappearing, ecologies perishing. Yep, we are in my 6th mass extinction event for sure. And it's their fault.

Mind you, if the humans all died, other life on me would flourish – just like it has before. I just wish they'd hurry up and go before they do too much damage to anyone or anything else. But I don't really like to see any species perish, so humans need to have a major rethink. They don't have to be the measure of all things – again, this is profound arrogance, imho. They need to rethink what it means to be human, in a world *not* of their own creation. They are not superior to everything else on, around and within me because everything was created equally, everything is as important and as necessary as the next thing, being or object. In fact, human bodies themselves are an entanglement of water, air, earth, a multitude of microorganisms, metals, other elements and even plastics – and they need to develop an acute understanding of their own animality and interrelatedness. They need to really understand that nature is not out there – it is within all creatures and things. Humans are nature too.

Indeed, the recent human experiences of this latest coronavirus has brought civilisation almost to its knees; thankfully, it looks like it is an object lesson in humility. Humans don't understand viruses, not really. Viruses are not living things. Viruses are complicated assemblies of molecules, including proteins, nucleic acids, lipids, and carbohydrates, but on their own they can't do anything until they enter a living cell. Without cells, viruses would not be able to multiply. So, as I said, viruses are not living things, but they need living things to live – and something like CHNOPS is both (inorganicially and organically or abiotically and biotically). In any case, humans are struggling with what they're calling COVID-19 (aka Coronavirus Disease 2019), but I'm welcoming it, because it's allowing me to take a breath.

Human Meet COVID-19; COVID-19 Meet Human

Yes Earth, **I am COVID-19**. I am at the epicentre of human life at this moment.

It's really not personal. I go where there is life. And CHNOPS gives me my life.

I have to say that humans are not a particularly good host. I much prefer bats, because they're super-hosts. I don't kill the bats. They don't even get sick from me. I don't hurt them – they're very clever in that they have adapted to co-exist with me. I have co-existed with bats (and birds) for 55 million years. And now you might ask, how? Well, it's because bats fly. There's a whole lot of complicated stuff that goes on at the cellular level, but it's flying that has allowed bats to adapt.[8] Humans will need to adapt too, in one way or another.

By the looks of it, it seems to me that I might just be what humans need. From what you're all saying – *Earth, Matter* and *CHNOPs* – humans are in trouble – real trouble. They think their latest trouble is because of me, but I don't think so. I have just made them STOP. Stand still! Slow down!

I wonder if humans are starting to rethink. Surely, they must be? Will they rethink themselves into a revolution to save themselves? Imagine that, little old me causing a revolution! I'm only miniscule, about 0.0001 of the width of a human hair[9] – but look at my power! The way I see it is if they don't learn to co-exist, then they're doomed! And I'll just keep co-existing with bats and birds, and that suits me fine.

My bat buddies tell me that humans are still eating them, which is rather puzzling to me. I'll say this simply humans, so you can understand it: *you eat the bat, you eat me.* And if you cage the bat next to other species (like pigs, cats, monkeys, snakes, pangolins) – well I will find life there too. After all, life is life to me. As I said, it's not personal!

Humans think they can eat anything or anyone – *that there is no limit.* There has been no other species on Earth that eats like humans do. They want it all, and by goodness, they've certainly had it all! The cruelty, suffering and killing is obscene – as if no other species matters. It's very interesting to me that nearly all human ancestors were vegetarians.[10] Now I'm not saying they all need to be vegans and vegetarians (*although most should be*), but they're not co-existing with other species. Those so-called *Western* humans (west of what?) are only just beginning to understand what companion species actually are.[11] You want my opinion? They really need to listen to their Indigenous brothers and sisters.

Gathering

"There's COVID-19 now", says Earth, gesturing towards CHNOPS and Matter.

"They're late", grumbles CHNOPS, cranky about being kept waiting. Matter feels responsible, and so keeps quiet – for now. CHNOPS is fairly hard to get along with at the best of times and Matter does not want to provoke them or they will all never hear the end of it.

"Well, they've been busy CHNOPS", says Earth, always the peacemaker. Earth has called this meeting because things are getting somewhat out of hand. They want to have a conversation with CHNOPS, Matter and COVID-19 because after all, they are an interesting contemporary ecology, entangled in and with each other, in fairly constant intra-action. And Earth is very concerned about the humans they are all affecting, and who are affecting all of them. It is time to get together for a talk.

As they all settle in for their conversation, COVID-19 finds themself very unsettled, and actually, a bit nervous. They feel very out of their depth and is not really sure why Earth has called for this gathering. However, COVID-19 thinks they will just listen deeply to what everyone else is saying. They are not very experienced at deep listening, but they will try very hard to do it.

Matter feels calm as always. They are fairly inert when it comes to most things and just got on with it. They did however understand concepts of reverence, respect, relationality and responsibility. There is a deep ecology at work here, a mutual ecology. In many ways they all rely upon each other, and all are as important as each other, no matter what CHNOPS thinks. They shared everything and all had their roles to play.

CHNOPS is annoyed at being kept waiting, but respects Earth's position that they are all in relation to each other. It isn't a cultural dynamic, but it is indeed cyclical and interrelated. Concepts of time, nature, and ancestry are ineffably entwined within and between them all, in a dialectical relationship in constant movement between past and future, experiential knowing and constant becoming. Despite CHNOPS' arrogance, they are fairly perceptive.

Earth settles down to speak and to listen. They are, all of them, connected by their common worlds, and their near constant state of becoming. They are certainly an ecology, in deep relation with all others, with the capacity to enhance or destroy all life and all things. And this is what worries Earth: the possibility of cataclysmic change.

As Earth settles into the group, prepared to listen deeply, to express themself, to move, to tell stories and share, they look at all of them: bombastic CHNOPS, the very active COVID-19, and the steady Matter, and thinks how positive it is that they all agree to come together. With this thought, they begin to speak.

Notes

1 'De' meaning 'from' in Spanish.
2 Barad (2007).
3 Stewart (2012).
4 Braidotti (2013).
5 Hird and Yusoff (2019, p. 272).
6 Yunkaporta (2019).
7 Yunkaporta (2019, p. 3, original emphasis).
8 Appolonia, Hunt and Schmitz (2020).
9 Cuffari (2020).
10 Dunn (2012).
11 Haraway (2008) and Latour (2004).

References

Appolonia, A., Hunt, B., & Schmitz, A. (2020). *Why bats can fight off so many viruses?* https://www.businessinsider.com/bats-breeding-ground-viruses-super-host-coronavirus-2020-4?r=AU&IR=T?utm_source=copy-link&utm_medium=referral&utm_content=topbar

Barad, K. (2007). *Meeting the universe halfway: Quantum physics and the entanglement of matter and meaning.* Duke University Press.

Braidotti, R. (2013). *The posthuman.* Polity Press.

Currari, B. (2020). *The size of SARS CoV2 compared to other things.* https://www.news-medical.net/health/The-Size-of-SARS-CoV-2-Compared-to-Other-Things.aspx

Cutter-Mackenzie-Knowles, A., Lasczik, A., Wilks, J., Logan, M., Turner, A., & Boyd, W. (2020). *Touchstones for deterritorialising socioecological learning: The Anthropocene, posthumanism and common worlds as creative milieux.* Palgrave Macmillan.

Dunn, R. (2012). Human ancestors were nearly all vegetarians. *Scientific American,* July, *23.*

Haraway, D. (2008). *When species meet*. University of Minnesota.

Hird, M. J., & Yusoff, K. (2019). Lines of shite – Microbial-mineral chatter in the Anthropocene. In R. Braidotti & S. Bignall (Eds.), *Posthuman ecologies: Complexity and process after Deleuze* (pp. 265–281). Rowman & Littlefield International.

Latour, B. (2004). *Politics of nature*. Harvard University Press.

Richardson, L. (2003). Writing: A method of inquiry. In N. Denzin & Y. Lincoln (Eds.), *Turning points in qualitative research: Tying knots in a handkerchief*. Altamira Press.

Stewart, K. (2012). Pockets. *Communication and Critical/Cultural Studies*, *9*(4), 365–368.

Yunkaporta, T. (2019). *Sand talk: How Indigenous thinking can save the world*. Text Publishing.

CHAPTER 2

Posthuman Arts-Based Experimentation through Place-as-Event

Amy Cutter-Mackenzie-Knowles, Alexandra Lasczik, Lisa Siegel and Tracy Young

Abstract

This chapter places learning in a posthuman experimentation. This posthuman experimentation engages 'place as event' extending from 'nature as event' as framed by Debaise (2017) and formerly by Deleuze (1980), Whitehead (1920) and James (1912). This process of working-through or experimenting attunes creatively to affect and the sensorial as a key engagement of socioecological learning through passages of poetry, photographic essay and creative writing. In effect, the posthumanist learner (re)adjusts to being already entangled as nature and not separated or dominated by humanist dispositions. In this process we acknowledge the everpresent and sometimes incomplete traces of the posthuman, socioecological learner.

Keywords

posthuman – nature as event – relationality – story – arts-based – visual essay

 DOI:10.1163/9789004507838_003

turn sharply to contemporary thinking
to the learning contours of posthumanism

every concept with an irregular contour
to ignite, expand or diffract learning
unsettling institutions to see, sense, think and act anew

learning is discovery, a heightened curiosity
learning is a constant process
of discovery,
of becomings
learning unfolds with thinking,
with creativity and
through social dilemma,
as nomadic, always moving,
inquiry into the not-yet-known

concepts to shift the image of thought in ways that are not
inflexible or fixed

place as event

articulate and agitate posthumanist learning
de-centre or deterritorialise

place as event

the posthumanist learner (re)adjusts
to being already entangled as

place as event

but you cannot recognise an event, because
when it is gone,
it is gone
each event is a passage
it is there,
it is here again

something is here again

an event is an accumulation of
uneventful relations and happenings
all is event within perception

the making and (dis)order of the world

place as event

uncovers praxis that unsettles anthropocentric
default perceptions of human superiority

ontologies of the multiple

when you know a thing,
to recognise that you know it, and
when you do not know a thing, to
recognise that you
do not know it
that is knowledge

learning is about the unknowable and silent
attuning with the affective, material and
unknown the relational and nuanced
complexities of learning
that requires a rethinking of ontology of
knowing and being
that embraces the collective process of

becoming-with
becoming worldly
and worlding

nature requires
children to be
children first;
the child is a metaphysical being
what children feel, see, hear, sense and imagine

the creatures in the lake
the conversation with a tree
the friendly support of a pedadog[1]

these invite practices of thinking-with

of acknowledging what is around and inside us,
before and after us
extending the connective tissue
of our relations,
our materiality
our collective memory overlaps
folding and
enfolding and
refolding with every
small ripple of affect with no specific time
or space
they are always
expanding and morphing

the posthumanist learner
has to feel and
sense to learn, using
experimental methods such as
relating with rivers, talking with trees, or
becoming speculative with lake creatures through stories,
poetry, art or deeper questions that put the quest of discovery into

learning;
this is
learning

that is not driven
by humanist cognitive thought or
language, but with emotion, embodiment
and affect

forwards to a lively Earth.

Posthuman Thought Experiments

> Thought experiments are devices of the imagination used to investigate the nature of things … The primary philosophical challenge of thought experiments is simple: How can we learn about reality (if we can at all), just by thinking? More precisely, are there thought experiments that enable us to acquire new knowledge about the intended realm of investigation without new empirical data? (Brown & Fehige, 2014, p. 1)

In response to Brown and Fehige's (2014) question, indeed there are thought experiments that enable humans to acquire new knowledge, but not necessarily without new observation or experience. A thought experiment lingers in the space between empiricism and theory. In this chapter, the thought experiments that linger in these liminal spaces are activated by arts-based educational research methods (Barone & Eisner, 2012). Specifically, we respond artfully to place – in this instance the place of a writing retreat in northern New South Wales, Australia by experimenting with role-play, swimming, walking, mapping and photography. This place not only beguiled us with its natural beauty, but was also the impetus for scholarship, collegiality and philosophical meanderings over the course of three days as we wrote and read and experienced and experimented. Conscious of its ancient and continuing sovereignty as Country of the Bundjalung Nation, specifically the Arakwal people, we acknowledge both its living history and its ongoing teachings, as well as our presence as guests. This place is now a tangible presence in our collective scholarship, and specifically in the work portrayed herein.

The focus of this exploration of thought experiments hinges on place, nature and the concept of event through the documented form of photography as visual essay, which extends through creative writing and poetry. Thus, the images and creative writings in this chapter not only portray posthuman thought experimentations with place-as-event, but they are also curated and positioned as critical visual texts (Cutcher et al., 2015; Lasczik Cutcher, 2018) and ought to be read as such, rather than as mere illustrations or figures. They are neither representative nor mimetic, but rather are artworks that operate critically in the slowing of the reading, in the lingering-with (Lasczik Cutcher & Irwin, 2017). We offer these three posthuman thought experiments that are grounded in and generated from the same place experience, as layered artworks that are open to myriad possible readings and mediated place experiences that unfold in the intertextualities between page and reader. In such a way, they operate as provocations for further posthuman thought experiments, as well as their own becomings.

Place as Event

> Nature as event … lays paths of thought and praxis by showing that conceptions of posthumanist learnings are incomplete or impartial and always moving in their becomings. (Young & Cutter-Mackenzie-Knowles, 2020, p. 3)

As Young and Cutter-Mackenzie-Knowles (2020) assert, such posthumanist experiments as we share here will always be partial, curtailed and unknowable. The architecture of engagement (Cutcher, 2015) in this chapter has thus been intentionally designed in order to give a *sense* of the live experience of place-as-event. This is because events are ephemeral, situated and experiential and any documentation or recording of such an event will accordingly be unavoidably incomplete, partial, limited. In the design of the reading where the reader is a proactive agent in the portrayal, we have sought to create a simulacrum of the experience we three authors had in this place-as-event. Such a simulacrum ineffably acknowledges our presence as outsiders, as guests on unceded sovereign territory. Offering such a portrayal both ignites and makes space for multiple readings and engagements.

Posthuman Thought Experiments

As we use our minds and our mouths and our hands gesturing to discuss posthumanist pedagogy; we unconsciously intra-act with the hot and moist air. Our faces become flushed and red, droplets of sweat trace across our necklines and down our spines. As our bodies heat, so do our brains – our words come out in bursts like flames leaping up out of a campfire, sizzling into the humid atmosphere around us.

Realising that our human bodies are reacting to the other-than-human heat, we decide to continue our discussion in the pool. We immerse ourselves and the wet materiality reminds us of our corporeality. Our affinity with the water also reminds us that we are kin. As the cool water lowers the temperature in our heads and our bodies, our words take on a flowing quality. Our conversation comes in waves instead of bursts, as one thought merges into another.

As we readjust ourselves to our cool embodied state, the relief turns into light bubbles of conversation about our relationship with water. About how, when we were young, our relationship to bodies of water was more one of trying to master it by moving through it at speed; whereas now the relationship with water is one of floating and immersion, surrender and joy.

Our talk about our relationships with water expands to relationships with other non-human entities. As educators and researchers, we rouse our colleagues to expand their pedagogies to include other-than-human entities, but to also grant them as much legitimacy as human entities.

How though?

We can never be a dolphin, a dragonfly, a drop of water; we can never presume to know their intentions or to speak in their voice. And yet this very human tendency to anthropomorphise appears over and over again in education and research as we vainly try to connect.

We note that interwoven through the chapter in the first book[2] *are examples of posthumanist pedagogical possibilities that don't anthropomorphise. A boy interviews a tree, and is content with the tree's silence instead of enlisting a classmate to speak as the tree, or to speak for the tree himself. Neither does anyone attempt to speak for Kosi the pedadog or for the Whanganui River, an entity granted its own personhood.*

As we continue to linger in our posthuman thinking, the cool begins to turn to cold as the breeze picks up, and our flowing words turn choppier as the wind whisks across our bodies and the water of the pool. We emerge into the still-warm air, and we re-immerse ourselves in the human retreat.

Experiment One: Amy

Dear Louise,

It is a little strange writing to a person I don't know and will never have the opportunity to know.

I came across your 'memorial walk' while on a writing retreat and I felt quite struck by our encounter. I set off on my walk with a purpose – 'to see, to feel, to sense shifting ecological relations'. At first I thought that to name a nature walk 'Louise's Walk' is overly humanistic, but I then I came to learn why, immediately shifting my thoughts to your story. You were so young to die – just 24 – only 8 years ago.

I decided to walk your walk keeping my purpose in/on my mind. I could sense you as I walked with ghostly materials scattered, almost sprinkled, along the journey. As I walked, I noticed I wasn't walking alone, as ants journeyed and brush turkeys spruiked. I slowed my pace, stood and watched. I wondered what it would be like to live as an ant, knowing I could never really know. And of course a fellow environmentalist or environmental educator would say that such wonder could quickly turn anthropomorphic. Why do humans get so undone by anthropomorphism, the placement of human values and attributes on other animals? It is relating – but we're told it is the wrong kind of relating.

The pavers and moss elegantly dance with no sense of sense, but my wonder is piqued as nature tightly holds, binds and traverses the red bricks. As I look deeply and then look, look and look again I see nature reclaiming Louise's Walk. Something tells me though that you would be OK with that, and I am reminded by the prose "And forget not that the Earth delights to feel your bare feet and the winds long to play with your hair". While your feet and hair are no longer here, your ghostly tracings linger through your walk. I sharply turn my mind again to what might your walk (Louise's Walk) look like in 100 years. What ghostly tracings will remain and shimmer?

Until next time,
Amy

LOUISE'S WALK

Experiment Two: Lisa

… walking in human/non-human nature …

> We must find another relationship to nature besides reification, possession, appropriation, and nostalgia. No longer able to sustain the fictions of being either subjects or objects, all the partners in the potent conversations that constitute nature must find a new ground for making meanings together. (Haraway, 2008, p. 158)

A paved path winds through a sub-tropical glade. Light filters down through glossy umbrellas of leaves and twisted grey mottled branches, to land like melted golden flakes on the leaf litter. We can hear birdsong overhead, and we catch a glimpse of the upright tail of a brush turkey scratching its way through the debris.

Deep breath.

A pristine primordial place.

Untouched by human hands?

We enter through a wooden arch – a slim tree trunk has wound itself around one of the supporting poles. The pole remains solemn and straight, while the trunk twists itself around that which used to be a living trunk, before being chopped down and placed again into the ground by one of the more recent human occupants of this land.

The gate swings open; a dried twig hangs. A composite leaf with opposite leaflets; the top leaflet is caught between the palings while the other leaflets float freely against the pale grey paint of the gate palings that almost, but not quite, match the pale grey of some of the surrounding tree trunks. A human chose the paint colour for the gate. How does a tree trunk know to colour itself grey and not pink, blue, or yellow?

A few steps in and a slight recoil as a long, lithe and black shape is caught in the corner of the eye. Not a snake after all, but a length of plastic piping that emerges out of the ground near the path, before arching gently over two tree roots, and disappearing under the leaf litter.

The path winds along, the different coloured pavers are bare in some spots, covered in moss in others. Concrete melts into forest, and the forest melts into concrete where a long dead leaf has imprinted itself. Another, freshly fallen leaf lies beside the ghostly tracings of its ancestor, still red and shapely and ignorant of its ultimate and inevitable demise.

Remembering we are nature, touched/untouched by the human hand, we walk down the path where wildness still reigns, but the detritus of human beings litters the landscape.

Experiment Three: Lexi

This walk becomes something else.

Four-year-old May takes my hand and leads me out the back door. She tells me she wants to walk with Louise. I allow myself to be led, and slowly we move down from the house, across the spongy carpet of grass and through the creaking gate to the path that is 'Louise's Walk'.

Moving with May slows me down, her little legs are not interested in a fast passage; she doesn't want this experience to be over too soon. She leans into the plants either side of the path at May height, smelling, looking, noticing and listening. We hear the loud rustling of the trees and branches and leaves, the deep croak of a sleepy frog woken by the recent rain, the chickens talking excitedly to each other as Katie throws the watermelon rind over the fence for them, back near the yard. We move deeper into the cool of the rainforest, slowly, lingering-with. The pace of our walk, the slow rhythm of our feet, our hearts, our eyes, compel an intense noticing, a deeper gaze. We are not just *with* nature: we *are* nature, amongst *other* nature.

May shows me a red leaf, some heart-shaped lichen, a small, grey ceramic plaque placed there, in the fork of a tree: Hope. I open a blue quandong and expose the green flesh. Its scent is fresh and clean, the taste bitter. I tell May that I've made jam from these berries, and she makes me promise to make some for her. We reach the end of Louise's Walk, and at the exit gate stands a post and lintel structure with a quote from the Prophet.[3]

May asks me to read it to her, and I say, again so gently, "My darling, it says this: 'Forget not that the earth delights to feel your bare feet and the winds long to play with your hair'".

May looks up at me, her big blue eyes so serious, and smiles before she skips all the way down the path and back to the house.

• • •

We return many times to this place together and apart, drawing out our connection with the site again and again, returning to our lingering-with in this special place, with flourishing plant and insect life, the mass-produced plastic and metal detritus now reclaimed by the living bush.

The rainforest looks so different fifty years on, and we have struggled to keep it at bay, away from the path, trying to preserve the trail in memorial for our dear Louise – but the moss has its own intention. It creeps and crawls on regardless, dominating the now-cracked and uneven pavers in an emerald velvety carpet.

This time, with this walk, May holds me close, her left hand on my left shoulder, my right hand in her right hand. I need her to help me walk this walk now, the dawdling pace a necessity, my feet frustratingly clumsy, my balance not what it was.

I'm worried I will fall but then May leads me, and we play our old game of 'blind mirror walk'. In this game, the one being led must do so with their eyes closed; it is a slow dance of trust.

I think of the first time we did this, an old memory now, when I found it so deeply confronting and did not want to lean into the space of dependency and promise, faith and custody. I was moved in my anxiety, to tears.

This time, I'm instantly transported forty years back, when I again walked this way, my arms closely around my mother, supporting her delicate passage as we moved into the church to farewell my Dad.

But this walk becomes something else.

May's arms around me make me feel safe and comforted and protected. "She won't let me fall", I think.

She leads me, my eyes closed and smiling, down the path as we have so many times before. May turns me to the right, tells me to bend from the waist, supporting me as I go, and adjusts the direction of my face, whispering, "Remember? We are learning as we look".

I open my eyes and smile. May has directed my gaze so that I am face-to-face with a glorious richly golden bloom. I inhale its fragrance deeply into my chest and again close my eyes, remembering.

The flower is a lily.

Closing

In *engaging* the posthuman in a suite of thought experiments *engaging* place-as-event and extending from 'nature as event' (Debaise, 2017; Deleuze, 1980; James, 1912; Whitehead, 1920), we have *engaged* a process of creatively and artfully working-through and working-with socioecological learning as passages of poetry, photographic essay and creative writing. Through these practices and engagements, we have reminded ourselves that at its most potent, learning through place-as-event is about discovery and experimentation, about thought in constant movement, as the not-yet-known unfolds through posthuman framing in a process of articulating socioecological deterritorializing. Whilst such learnings acknowledge the entanglements with the everpresent human learner, they also seek a decentring of humanism, troubling this tension by unsettling anthropocentric default perceptions through ontologies of multiplicity, of artfulness and of imagination. Socioecological learning through place, event, affect and the sensorial attunes to relationality, the complex and the unknown through materiality and experience, discovery and feel. It is within such a dynamic that posthuman socioecological learners are able to experience their own becomings-with through a flattened ontological positioning that embraces the collective and collaborative processes of experience and experimentation.

Notes

1 To more fully engage with this stanza, it is helpful to read the original chapter.
2 Cutter-Mackenzie et al. (2020).
3 Kahlil Gibran.

References

Barone, T., & Eisner, E. W. (2012). *Arts-based research*. New Sage.

Brown, J. R., & Fehige, Y. (2014). Thought experiments. In E. N. Zalta (Ed.), *The Stanford encyclopedia of philosophy*. http://plato.stanford.edu/archives/fall2014/entries/thought-experiment/

Cutcher, A. J. (2015). *Displacement, identity and belonging: An arts-based, auto/biographical portrayal of ethnicity & experience*. Sense Publishers.

Cutcher, A., Rousell, D., & Cutter-Mackenzie, A. (2015). Findings, windings and entwinings: Cartographies of collaborative walking and encounter. *International Journal of Education through Art, 11*(3), 449–458.

Cutter-Mackenzie, A., Lasczik, A., Boyd, W., Logan, M., Turner, A., & Wilks, J. (2020). *Touchstones for deterritorializing socioecological learning: The Anthropocene, posthumanism and commonworlds as creative milieux.* Palgrave Macmillan.

Debaise, D. (2017). *Nature as event: The lure of the possible*. Duke University Press.

Deleuze, G. (1980). *The logic of sense* (M. Lester & C. Stivale, Trans.). Columbia University Press.

James, W. (1912). *Essays in radical empiricism*. Longmans.

Lasczik Cutcher, A., & Irwin, R. L. (2017). Walkings-through paint: A c/a/r/tography of slow scholarship. *Journal of Curriculum and Pedagogy, 14*(2). doi:10.1080/15505170.2017.1310680

Whitehead, A. (1920). *The concept of nature: Tarner lectures delivered in Trinity College November 1919*. Cambridge University Press.

Young, T., & Cutter-Mackenzie-Knowles, A. (2020). Posthumanist learning: Nature as event. In A. Cutter-Mackenzie-Knowles, A. Lasczik, W. Boyd, M. Logan, A. Turner, & J. Wilks (Eds.), *Touchstones for deterritorializing socioecological learning: The Anthropocene, posthumanism and common worlds as creative milieux.* Palgrave Macmillan.

CHAPTER 3

Walking the Mandala

A Big-Little Way of Being and Knowing in Disrupted Worlds

Raoul Adam, Thilinika Wijesinghe, Yaw Ofosu-Asare and Philemon Chigeza

Abstract

Global disruptions can inspire new ways of teaching and thinking through the big questions of little things. Recognising our disrupted times, we explore the mandala as an integrative symbol – a visuo-spatial abstraction of a worldview – that invites and represents responses to big questions in ontology, cosmology, epistemology, axiology and eschatology. We re-imagine the mandala as an expansion and a contraction of intersecting 'opposites' (e.g. sacred-profane, mythos-logos, order-chaos) that can push-and-pull thinking through the wicked problems of disrupted times.

We embrace *Walking the Mandala* as a mytho-poetical and logico-mathematical act for learning and unlearning. It is at once an embodied and affective act of creative turns and qualitative diffractions, and a cognitive act of critical and analytical cartography that orientates and measures. It is a *circumambulation* – a circling of possibilities that connects oneself to others.

Finally, we introduce a novel three-dimensional mandala – the *Zygo* – as a material artefact and architecture for critical, creative and consilient thinking through disruptions in big-little worlds.

Keywords

mandala – symbolism – worldview – consilience

• • •

> Mandala [n]. Sanskrit. maṇḍala मंडलः 'circle', 'completion'. A generic term for any plan, chart or geometric pattern that represents the cosmos metaphysically or symbolically.
>
> New World Encyclopedia

DOI:10.1163/9789004507838_004

• • •

> The mandala serves a conservative purpose – namely, to restore a previously existing order. But it also serves the creative purpose of giving expression and form to something that does not yet exist, something new and unique. The second aspect is perhaps even more important than the first, but does not contradict it.
>
> Franz, cited in Jung & Franz (1964, p. 225)

∴

The Mandala: Big Questions and Little Things

Figure 3.1 Thanga painting of Manjuvajra mandala (Google Cultural Institute, public domain, https://commons.wikimedia.org/w/index.php?curid=35352478)

This chapter originated from a writing retreat in Northern New South Wales in early 2019. It is the creative extension of an earlier critical article on the unlearning of binary oppositions in the Anthropocene (Adam, Stevenson, Whitehouse & Chigeza, 2020). Both pieces were written in a milieu that is recognised as one of the most disrupted in modern history. *Trumpism*, *Brexit*, *Cambridge Analytica*, *Climate Change*, *Fake News*, *Me-Too*, *Black Lives Matter* and *COVID-19* are defining terms for these tumultuous times.

Perhaps every generation experiences itself as the most disrupted. Notwithstanding, in times of heightened disruption we tend to ask ourselves anew the biggest questions of ontology, cosmology, epistemology, eschatology and axiology: Who are we? How did we get here? How do we know? Where are we going? And, what should we do? Revisiting big questions requires new models and minds, a willingness to unlearn cherished answers that have failed, and the humility to revisit old answers that have been forgotten. Big questions reveal themselves in little things, like the fleeting intersections of our (the authors') lives.

At the time of the writing retreat, one of our authors (Raoul) was working on a pedagogical artefact (i.e. the *Zygo*) – the extension of a framework for Big-Little Thinking (BLT) – that can be used to facilitate mixed-methods explorations of contested issues. The artefact was based on the author's theory of Bi-relational Development (i.e. Adam, 2016) as a synthesis of the archetypal dynamics of 'eastern' mandalas and 'western' studies of cognitive-epistemological development. Our second author (Thilinika) – a PhD student from Sri Lanka – had lived experience, a research interest and artistic flair for Indian and Sri Lankan mandalas and the associated concept of *Chakravala* – meaning a cosmic disc or wheel (Shakya, 2000). A fortuitous seating arrangement over lunch led to a convergence of thoughts on the meanings of mandalas in disrupted times. This convergence was further revealed by a short walk around the house and grounds of the retreat. The house and grounds were decorated with an eclection of mandala-like mosaics, tiles, sculptures, weavings, artwork and architecture (Figure 3.2). A later interview with the owner-builder of the house provided some insight into how this eclection of mandalas came together. We include fragments from this conversation (House of Mandalas) as a glimpse into the ways that mandalas weave the archetypes of big questions into the little things of lives.

Some weeks after the retreat, a fortuitous meeting in a concrete university office overlooking the Pacific Ocean, wove our third author into the tapestry of the chapter. Yaw Ofosu-Asare – a PhD student and designer recently arrived from Ghana – introduced us to the *Adinkra*. The Adinkra are symbols literally woven into the fabric and imprinted into the artefacts of Ghanaian culture to convey complex meanings, knowledge and wisdom. Struck by the similarity of motifs between the Adinkra, Sri Lankan manifestations of the mandala, and the design of the Zygo – the three of us continued to *walk the mandala* together.

The following section is a collection (or diffraction) of mytho-poetical images and imagery that document our intersecting paths around through the mandala in disrupted times. Here, we bring into focus the eclecticism of little things – the splintered images and fragments of memory that dance freely into and between the symmetries of the mandala.

Figure 3.2 Montage of images and imagery from the location of the authors' writing retreat

House of Mandalas (Jayne – the owner of the property)

Creativity. Inspired by nature
Papua New Guinea
We lived on Islands.
Threads that open up. The house has earthy tones.
We made the mud bricks
Lived in the Kimberly in Aboriginal communities
Aboriginal connections in the house
Creativity and expression
We bring to a space.
The Cartwheel – a window on the wall.
Europe. Asia. Laos. We're gypsies.
Wherever we've been. We bring a little bit back.
Threads of material. Woven. Weaving.

Beautiful big wooden piece
A Mandala from the Burmese border.
Eyes are open
Stopped in a Songthaew. Soldiers.
Fear in the eyes of the people

Craftmanship. Bring light into the space
The wheel. Circular. Flowing.

The staircase
A spider-web. Weaving up. Weaving down.

The Butterfly mosaic – Birdwing
A quiet space – reforested
Cocooning – the new life
Metamorphosis – rising out – cycle of life

Art from the Kimberly
The Boab. The life source.
Devastation in the communities. Falls creek.
So many losses.
Being whole-hearted. Present.
Freeing ourselves.
Words in my head that I can't write.

[The rotunda] To balance the rectangles and squares.
A humble structure. Prayer. Meditation Room.
Catholic background.
Spirituality. To be in touch with our deepest self.
To feel you have all the answers is a very sad thing.

The arch. The Lotus flower.
To bring many things together.

Africa. Moroccan Tiles. Papuan Baskets.
Things that please your eyes – that feel connected
A mat in the yoga room. Design is circular
An Ashram in India.
Peoples' journeys.

Disappearing at the Joins (Raoul)

Saturdays swum in cool creeks swung with vines
Sunday's singing smiles wiped away by
Sermons dripping blood and judgment
Through years of hooded learning.

The Saints in black and white
Hid the sinful greys of colour in the
Mass of frankincense and frangipani.
Fruit-bats screeching through the hellfire sky
Sugarcane ashes alight upon my forehead.

Signs of the Cross.
Marks of the Beast.

Everywhere the Baphomet travelled and enravelled in
The yellow dots and lines of the Gunggandji bark
And the pentagrammic shirts of my metal-headed mate.
I caught it catching dreams on the Navajo plains
Saw it in the blue-red threads of Incan shawls
And the reed-green weaves of Botswanan bowls
On carvings in a longhouse walled in Bornean jungle
And dancing in the choking rings of Kayan refugees

A mandala on the wall of a Cambodian cave
Squaring the circle in a candled corner shining light
Along the Via Dolorosa to the Sepulcher's dome
A Chi-Rho cross on a Constantinian sun
In the Labyrinth of Notre Dame
And the marbled motifs on a mosque in Oman
Circled in the temple of Megiddo
Knotted in the Byzantine mosaics of Nebo
Then hewn in carvings strewn in sacred gorges
And petroglyphs flung at the End of the World
Circles. Crosses. Dots.
Tesseracts and hyperspheres
Disappearing at the joins.

Dawning slowly

Two in a zero
A million in one.
All mythos. All logos.
All science. All art.
All nature. All culture.
That walked me here.

Figure 3.3 Montage of images from Raoul Adam's walkings in Jordan, Oman & Israel

Circling the Adinkra (Yaw)

The circle. How can so many meanings be ascribed to one shape?
Sun. Moon. Earth.
All circular.
The recurrent symbol of the Adinkra.
Designs of my Ghanaian heritage.
I understood its meanings.
Until now.
Far from home I saw the Mandalas of South Asia.
And understood the Adinkra again for the first time.
Wonder. Interconnection.
The ubiquitous circle.
What philosophies reside?

What aphorisms hide?
I seek within its fold?
A simple symbol speaks my truth. Replicates my world.
The biggest questions.
In little things.
Intense emotions.
Symbols shaping understandings.
I am a citizen of the world.
Conflicted between African and Western ideas
An age-old battle. Faith and Reason. Raging in the little things.

Rent. Torn apart. Undone.

Then the symbols speaking wisdom from the fabric torn.

Knotted. Together. One.

The beauty of symbols.
Abstract natures in aesthetical complexities
Clarity and connection to nature, to being, to humanity.
I have searched the symbols of the Adinkra, Alchemy, Ashtamangala, Astrology, Aztec, Chakra, Celtic, Lakota Sioux, Norse, and Mu Lemurian.
All together
Moving parts.
A circled core.

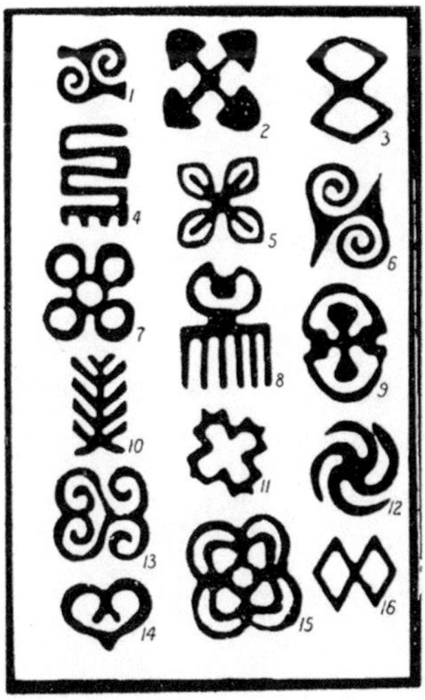
1
2
3
4
5
6
7
8
9
10
11
12
13
14
15
16

Figure 3.4 Adinkra (from Rattray, 1927, p. 265; public domain, https://commons.wikimedia.org/w/index.php?curid=14895335)

Figure 3.5 1825 Adinkra cloth (public domain, http://www.museumkennis.nl/lp.rmv/museumkennis/i001580.html)

Encounters (Thilinika)

Encounter I

Meetings, conferences, discussions
The longer they run, the less my concentration
Paper, pencil or pen
Scribbling something from within
Circles filling blank sheets
At first no meanings
Then practised, drawn and painted.

Everything has a beginning?
Interactions and intra-actions
Blur the lines and turn them inwards.

Encounter II

I moved to India for my first degree
Drawing stilled me
Mehendi hand on hand

Circling still but filling with designs
Inscribed on temple walls and minds
Everywhere the circle and the knot

Mandala

The circle of Sinhala and Hindi
Layering, spreading, expanding, opening.
Unfolding, shrinking, negating, closing.
Everything and nothing in the void
Who, what, where, and how am I?

Encounter III

Returning to Sri Lanka,
The circled drawings are a part of me.
Set in stone and rising like the Sandakadapahana (moonstone)
Entrance to an Ancient Kingdom
Entrance to a modern self

Samsara

My bare eyes cannot see clearly.

Encounter IV

Arriving in Australia
The Mandala there before me
Circling Western Malls
Woven through the market stalls
Students colouring circles in the library
To escape the stress of study.
A retreat.
A meeting of minds
In the language of mandalas
And of western science
Words and numbers
Numbers and pictures
Without a trace of contradiction.
Learning and unlearning circles

Walking the Mandala

Marking the end.
Is it the beginning of the end?
Confusion is what we grapple with
Expressed through art in journeys
Peace and masterpieces.
Not one. Many.
Many as one.
One as many.

Encounter V

A third encounter with design.
The student from Ghana
His ideas in my drawings
Every penciled movement. Every shape.
A book of Australian Aboriginal Art
Mandalas in the dots and lines
I saw and drew them in familiar shapes
Context and meaning in artistic expansions.
Lost in Space. Matter. Time.
To be found?
To be fulfilled?

Mytho-Mathematical Mandala (Raoul, Thili, Yaw)

We present the mandala as an integrative symbol for disrupted times that welcomes the poet and the mathematician, the storyteller and the scientist, with equal warmth and measure. Our hope is that walking the mandala will encourage educators to explore new pedagogies to bring mytho-poetical and logico-mathematical ways of knowing and being to bear on complex problems. Walking is an act of fusion – body and mind – practice and theory – poetry and motion – order and chaos. So far, we have walked the mandala through mytho-poetical images and fragments of memory. This imagery – often diffracted and opaque – expresses the creative messiness of lives and little things. In some ways, this chapter is part of a book that celebrates creativity and the diffraction in an educational milieu too often dominated by naïvely monolithic expressions of the convergent and the replicative.

The mandala is a *simplex* symbol – simple and complex. It can be full of colours or blacks and whites; labyrinthine designs or straight lines; eternities and infinities or beginnings and ends. It can be painstakingly created or destroyed and swept away, with equal reverence. The rhizomatic elements need not kneel within the symmetries of Mandalas. As authors, we have not recalled our memories in poetic forms merely to reduce them to more analytic prose or *restore a previously existing order*. The symmetry of the Mandala *depends* upon its chaos. Why draw a circle if there's nothing to contain? Why draw a bigger circle if nothing can escape? Why draw a circle at all, or a square or a line that divides? Why plot a number or find a better word? Living breathes chaos and order just the same. The more we impose our order, the more we expose our chaos. The more we impose our chaos, the more we expose our order. The mandala is both-and-either-or-neither-nor and in-between.

Here, we seek to disrupt the logico-mathematical impulse – at least in its dominant western form – to reject the mandala as a primitive symbol for 'alternative types' who are too prone to poetry or colouring-in. This impulse is completely right about half the truth. Conversely, we also seek to disrupt the mytho-poetical impulse – at least in its dominant western form – to occlude the mandala from the art of science and numbers. This impulse too, is completely right about half the truth. Our mytho-mathematical act is to walk the mandala with words and numbers, art and science, mythos and logos. Our rationale is that disrupted worlds are usually worlds unfairly divided and naively bifurcated on the deepest levels – masculine and feminine, sacred and profane, nature and culture, subjective and objective, art and science. The mandala invites these 'opposites' into a common space.

The invitation to step into the common space of the mandala is not one to be taken lightly, especially in disrupted times with fractured sides. As a symbol of peace – the mandala must be fought for. Its circle is a ring where sides will enter war and fight each other close to death, before realising their wounds are self-inflicted. The real war is won in walking the circle that starts and ends all wars – a *circumambulation*. Accordingly, we present a unique mandala for disrupted worlds – the Zygo.

Zygo

> All models are wrong, but some are useful. (George Box)

Zygo means 'pair' or 'union' from the Ancient Greek word ζυγόν (zugón) meaning yoke (e.g. Subjective-Objective). The Zygo is a mandala-like model to facilitate the teaching and learning of critical, creative and consilient thinking about the clash of worldviews that characterise times of disruption. It is an artefact of a framework for critical, consilient and creative thinking about controversial problems and issues. Its contours, folds, faces and nodes encourage penetrative conversations through 'wicked problems'.

In some ways, the Zygo represents a way to think *about* the Left-Right Spectrum (LRS) so implicit in the framing of problems, as much as from it. The LRS is a prevalent construct in the representation of issues that arise in disrupted times. In its exclusively linear and oppositional forms (←—→) the LRS teaches us to be left or right, traditional or progressive, masculine or feminine, mythopoetical or logico-mathematical, and critical or creative – for once and for all. Perhaps worse, are cosmographies that present left and right as up (positive +) and down (negative –) – for once and for all. As a form of mandala, the Zygo complicates, curves, enfolds and multiplies linear representations of the LRS as a straight and double-ended arrow. Accordingly, it is one response to the growing recognition of the need for metaphysical models, maps and metaphors to make meaning of the wicked problems that accompany an age of disruption (e.g. Bawden, 2010, 2011a, 2011b; Brainard, 2017; Gardner, 2004; Godfrey-Smith, 2006; Henriques, 2003; McGilchrist, 2009; Mueller, 2016; Ross-Holst, 2004).

Metaphysical maps – like mandalas – offer particularly abstract orientations to the complex terrains of social issues, just as geographical maps offer abstract orientations to material terrains. They frame the equivalent poles, latitudes, longitudes and contours of worldviews and can be populated by infinite combinations of 'little things' – the lived experiences and everyday manifestations of abstractions. Indeed, we can use such cartographic terms to summarise the Zygo, albeit with an expanded metaphysical terrain.

Specifically, the Zygo is a multi-dimensional mandala in the abstract form of an emergent hyper-cube (i.e. tesseract) or hyper-sphere (Figure 3.6). Like an archetypal mandala – its symmetry proceeds (*recedes*) from an infinitesimal

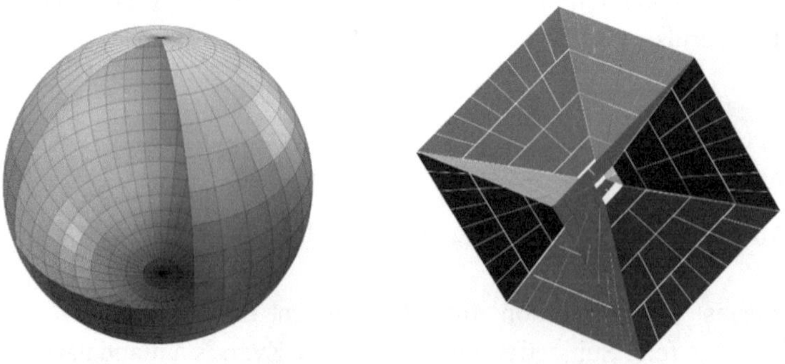

Figure 3.6 Visio-spatial representation of Zygo as hyper-sphere and hyper-cube (tesseract)

point and expands (*contracts*) into exponentially more complex (*simple*) forms arranged in ever-proceeding (*receding*) spacetime. Collectively, the Zygo's six sides or *frames* map intersections of *Problems* and *Solutions* through *Matter*, *Mind, Mood* and *Meaning* as different (*same*) dimensions of the same (*different*) thing. The contiguity of these frames draws thinking about problems and solutions into the ambiguous 'space' at the 'centre' of the hypercube – a *Meta Frame.*

PROBLEMS are usually experienced as something as broken, missing, unbalanced or misaligned. The problem frame encourages clearer and more connected identification of problems. It helps to show that one problem usually has many sub-problems and related problems. The Zygo represents chronological and spatial layers of a problem in order to encourage thinking about its context, entanglement with other problems, and the many ways of representing a situated problem through time and across disciplines.

MATTER emphasises the subject and content (i.e. substance) of thinking. It uses macro and micro scales of space and time to ask the 'who, what, when and where' of an issue. *Matter* is mapped through the thresholds of a 'Big History' which swirls with 'things' (mineral, vegetable, animal) and their incalculable interactions within and across the fractured layers of space and time. It is the existential 'stuff' reflected and created in our maps – always shifting, spinning and reconfiguring between the lines of mind and meaning we overlay.

MIND emphasises the ways we think and know about *matter*. It asks 'how' we know and is mapped by lines and layers that represent the gradations between our most basic mental categories – *dyads* – those poles of perennial and ubiquitous *spectra* that are often (mis)named in reference to their framing poles as 'opposites' (e.g. masculine-feminine, subjective-objective, open-closed). The Zygo's mapping of the lines of mind gives a twist and full turn to the Likert Scales and arrows of western thinking. The Zygo's lines of mind can be mapped and measured to bi-polar scales and Likert Scales, but they also represent the circularity, recursivity, relationality and consilience of poles.

MOOD emphasises the affective and emotive dimension of life. As a dimension of the Zygo it aims to revalue affectivity and explore the entanglements of mood and matter, feelings and judgements, emotion and reason. As a side of the tesseract and a dimension of the Zygo, mood challenges the assumed primacy and separation of cognition and language in the making of meaning and the approach to problems.

MEANING emphasises the ways we value and evaluate *matter* in the presence of mind and mood. It explores 'why' we construct and ascribe value to the matter we have in mind. Meaning represents the ascription of positive and negative value to Matter.

SOLUTIONS are any coordination, configuration or creation of parts that help to address a problem. A solution is usually framed as a statement that identifies something as helping, fixing or balancing. The solution frame encourages clearer and more connected identification of solutions. It helps to reveal that one solution usually has many sub-solutions and related solutions. It can also reveal that some 'solutions' create problems and some 'problems' create solutions. The *solution* frame is always negotiated through other frames. What may appear as a solution at one layer that resolves intense *moods* and even violence, can be shown to have origins in a solution involving a simple distribution of *matter* at another layer. Relatedly, this simple solution of distribution may be related to a solution of *mind* arising from a related context. The Zygo encourages multiple frames, twists and turns – in the act of coordination towards solutions.

The *META FRAME* represents the ubiquitous but ambiguous origin of all other frames. Like the recursive origin and extremity of the mandala, it invites and defies speculation, demands reverence and incites profanity, and exposes the subjectivity of our most objective efforts. It could be nothing. It could be everything. Most importantly, the Meta Frame disrupts and exposes the necessary subjectivity and cultural embeddedness of the Zygo's form. It encourages diffractions, transmogrifications and new representations. It deliberately invites new forms that seriously and playfully move away from, or even construct themselves through, the Zygo's deceptively straight lines, fixed angles, and numbered frames. There are rivers flowing, roots growing, leaves falling, waves crashing, and sand dunes blowing throughout these lines. There are endless colours too – imaginable beneath the pragmatic printings of 0,0,0s and 255, 255, 255s.

This intersecting architecture of Matter, Mind, Mood and Meaning and their convergence-emergence in relation to a meta-frame, provides reference points for relational navigation between seemingly conflicting worldviews. We explore the specific architectures of the Zygo and related theory (e.g., Adam 2016) elsewhere in more formal prose. Our intention here is only to provide a multimodal glimpse of its affinity with the mandala as a metaphysical map that can be walked, talked and taught in different ways to explore the great disruptions expressed in little things.

Our task resonates with Walcott's (2006) observation of the cosmogram:

> As portrayed in mandalas, cosmograms (depictions of the universe as an ordered and harmonious system) employ a spatial visualization that falls into a different category from the currently contentious cartographic camps of positivists, realists, postmodernists, social theorists, and others.

> By directing visualization to the interior spaces of the observer's mind, this device contributes a non-Western perspective on the two-dimensional mapping of physical space with its portrayal of metaphysical, multidimensional experiential space. (p. 73)

However, we are eager to observe the implicit chaos in harmonies and to integrate, rather than isolate, these camps of Western cartographies. Walking the Zygo as mandala can be an ethnomathematical journey. Its straight lines can lead to curving paths. Its flattened faces can bring weathered voices into conversation. Its nodes and networks can be sketched with stories and symbols and then erased.

Models and architectures have great educational value in disrupted times and lives. Educators are significant facilitators (or inhibitors) of social exchanges that may benefit from 'big picture' models as ways of representing, theorising, meditating and playing within the tensions manifest in disrupted times. Gardner (2004) goes so far as to consider instituting 'psychological studies of the synthesizing or interdisciplinary mind' (p. 250) to facilitate – among other capabilities – 'Knowledge of and ability to interact civilly and productively with individuals from quite different cultural backgrounds – both within one's own society and across the planet' (p. 254). The Zygo is an attempt to synthesise the mytho-poetical form of the mandala with the logico-mathematical and analytical modalities of formal education. This is a consilient act – an act of bringing together seemingly incommensurate modalities. As Wilson (1998) acknowledges, there are significant implications for a more consilient approach to the study of social issues:

> Most of the issues that vex humanity daily – ethnic conflict, arms escalation, over population, abortion, environment, endemic poverty, to cite several most persistently before us – cannot be solved without integrating knowledge from the natural sciences with that of the social sciences and humanities. (p. 13)

Consilient approaches require representations that cross, or at least invite a crossing of disciplinary boundaries, whilst retaining the meanings within them.

Constructing representations that cross disciplinary boundaries is the task of a scholar. Communicating representations across disciplinary boundaries is the task of a teacher. A fundamental challenge for educators is the effective representation and exploration of relational meanings, especially those involving complex interactions between beliefs and values in psychological, social, cultural, political life. This challenge is well-acknowledged in the call for education for 'soft skills' and 'twenty-first century skills' to produce and manage knowledge in a complex and contested world. The representation and facilitation of these soft skills by educators presents a technical problem with a mechanical and conceptual dimension. The problem concerns if and how soft skills can be represented and facilitated through the hard technologies of educational apparatus. Without hard technologies and educational apparatus, the teaching of soft skills tends to be limited to qualitative modalities (e.g. stories and soft symbols). The technical conceptual problem concerns the need for an educational system and method that is simple enough to be communicable, yet able to generate and represent great complexity of thinking in-and-across domains of knowledge.

The Zygo offers a way to teach soft skills through its unique mix of modalities. As a visual symbol, model and map, it can be used and adapted in a range of learning contexts combining novelty, curiosity, play, and metacognition to engage diverse learners.

Conclusion (*Beginning*)

We have concluded this chapter with glimpses of the Zygo as a novel mandala. As noted at the outset, our disrupted milieu is marked by a common discourse of polarised responses to Trumpism, Brexit, AI, Climate Change, and most recently a global pandemic – all in a *post-truth* world. These are big issues and the development of the Zygo as an artefact has facilitated our thinking and teaching about them. It is a development that has necessarily crossed disciplinary borders and ideological lines. We have found that the biggest questions of socio-politico-religious issues reside in the smallest choices about the colour, material, shape, size and symmetry of an object. This realisation and the process of big-little thinking encourages our ongoing project to position mandalas in all their forms as important sites for contemplation, communication and navigation through disrupted times. Mandalas as maps and metaphors can help us to seek common meanings through abstractions in times of war with each other and within ourselves. They beckon us to walk the lines of mythos and logos until they disappear in the circumambulation that brings us back together. They draw us in and push us out to exchange the blinding binding lines of symmetry for the creative chaos of little things. We walk the mandala. And so, for now, we walk away.

References

Adam, R. (2016). *Education for wicked problems and the reconciliation of opposites: A theory of bi-relational development*. Routledge.

Adam, R., Whitehouse, H., Stevenson, R. B., & Chigeza, P. (2020). The socioecological (un)learner: Unlearning binary oppositions and the wicked problems of the Anthropocene. In A. Cutter-Mackenzie-Knowles, A. Lasczik, J. Wilks, M. Logan, A. Turner, & W. Boyd (Eds.), *Touchstones for deterritorializing socioecological learning: The Anthropocene, posthumanism and common worlds as creative milieux* (pp. 49–74). Palgrave Macmillan.

Artress, L. (1996). *Walking a sacred path: Rediscovering the labyrinth as a spiritual practice.* Penguin Publishing Group.

Bawden, R. J. (2010). Messy issues, worldviews and systemic competencies. In C. Blackmore (Ed.), *Social learning systems and communities of practice* (pp. 89–101). Springer.

Bawden, R. J. (2011a). Epistemic aspects of social ecological conflict. In D. Wright, C. E. Camden-Pratt, & S. B. Hill (Eds.), *Social ecology: Applying ecological understanding to our lives and our planet*. Hawthorn Press.

Bawden, R. J. (2011b). Social ecologies in conflict: The clash of epistemes and the challenge of the modern. In D. Wright, C. Camden-Pratt, & S. Hill (Eds.), *Social ecology: Applying ecological understanding to our lives and our planet* (pp. 52–63). Hawthorn Press.

Brainard, S. F. (2017). *Reality's fugue: Reconciling worldviews in philosophy, religion and science*. Pennsylvania State University Press.

Gardner, H. (2004). How education changes: Considerations of history, science, and values. In M. M. Suarez-Orozco & D. B. Qin-Hillard (Eds.), *Globalization: Culture and education in the new millennium* (pp. 235–258). University of California Press.

Godfrey-Smith, P. (2006). Theories and models in metaphysics. *The Harvard Review of Philosophy*, *14*. doi:10.5840/harvardreview20061411

Henriques, G. (2003). The tree of knowledge system and the theoretical unification of psychology. *Review of General Psychology*, *7*(2), 150–182. doi:10.1037/1089-2680.7.2.150

Jung, C. G., & Franz, M.-L. (1964). *Man and his symbols*. Dell Pub. Co.

McGilchrist, I. (2009). *The master and his emissary*. Yale University Press.

Mueller, A. (2016). Beyond ethnographic scriptocentrism: Modelling multi-scalar processes, networks, and relationships. *Anthropological Theory*, *16*(1), 98–130.

New World Encyclopedia. (2020). *Mandala*. https://www.newworldencyclopedia.org/entry/Mandala

Rattray, R. S. (1927). *Religion and art in Ashanti.* Clarendon Press.

Ross-Holst, C. (2004). Preface. In M. M. Suarez-Orozco & D. B. Qin-Hillard (Eds.), *Globalization: Culture and education in the new millennium* (pp. ix–xi). University of California Press.

Shakya, M. (2000). Basic concepts of mandala. *Voice of History*, *15*(1), 81–88.

Walcott, S. M. (2006). Mapping from a different direction: Mandala as sacred spatial visualization. *Journal of Cultural Geography*, *23*(2), 71–88.

Wilson, E. O. (1998). *Consilience: The unity of knowledge*. Knopf.

CHAPTER 4

The Risky Socioecological Learner

Jemma Peisker, Ben Ryan, Billy Ryan and Ziah Peisker

Abstract

This chapter seeks to enact socioecological portrayals of risk through artful thought experiments. Through scaffolded and considered risky activities, students and children are able to practise the skills to manage risks, exercise judgement and responsibility, and take the lead in their own learning processes. In a time where risk aversion culture is prevalent in schools, young people need exposure to scaffolded reasonable risk-taking activities to improve decision making and cope with unexpected events. As parents and educators, we have the opportunity to motivate children and students to engage 'risk' (and failure) as an opportunity to grow, and develop grit and resilience. This chapter captures the experiences of two teacher-parents as they embrace the risky business of teaching, and their two student-teenage-children as they encounter the risky business of learning. The form of this chapter, in its arts-based experimental portrayals that include the voices of young people, could also be considered a risk in academic publishing. Yet as the activities and the experimental presentation of this chapter reveals, when risks are calculated, and young people allowed their agency, socioecological learning flourishes.

Keywords

risk in education – socioecological learning – outdoor education – nature-based learning – child-framed

Living in and Challenging a Risk Adverse Culture

Wilks et al. (2020) established that the risk aversion experienced in wider society is also experienced in the field of education. Causes of risk aversion in education such as neoliberal structures, litigation, educational trends, and the risk preferences of teachers manifests as a "range of negative consequences for students" (Wilks et al., 2020, p. 83) and influences the quality of learning experiences for students with which to engage. In the mix of risk adverse culture in education, is

DOI:10.1163/9789004507838_005

the marginalisation of the connectedness of 'nature and children' where risks are positioned as obstacles to nature-based learning (Wilks et al., 2020).

In their chapter, the *Risky Socioecological Learner* Wilks et al. (2020, p. 84) argued that when risks are positioned as obstacles to nature-based learning opportunities, learners are disembodied from their nature-learning experiences, endangering "the future of environmentalism, sustainable design enterprise and the planetary health of the Earth." In this chapter we posit that it is essential that learners are empowered to be able to "develop, innovate and express themselves and their identity in nature-based settings" (Wilks et al., 2020, p. 84).

The unique position of the first two authors of this chapter, one as a Principal of a regional school, the other a university academic, and both as teachers and parents, brings new meanings and entwinings to the concept discussed in Wilks et al.'s (2020) chapter, of *in loco parentis* (in place of the parent) in exercising risk aversion in education. In this context part of our roles as risky socioecological parent-teachers is understanding the perspectives and experiences of the learner through our own familiarity and proficiency of 'risky' tasks. The first two authors use boundaries, scaffolded risks and supported failures in nature-education as an opportunity for their student-teenage-children to learn and grow in skill, resilience, confidence and courage. Additionally, in an age of increased screen time resulting in decreased nature time (Oswald et al., 2020), and detrimental effects of passive redundant entertainment (Csikszentmihalyi, 2014), outdoor nature-learning and placed-based education provides physical, active engagement that we view as essential to young bodies and minds.

The images and words of the student-teenage-children demonstrate the valuable and vital business of risky socioecological learning to their mind-set and physical enthusiasm. The student-teenage-children also took risks in their written expressions for this chapter, in both their chosen prose and communication format, which varies from the risks the parent-teachers took with their own words and stories. Particularly significant for appreciating the risky business of socioecological learning, is the student-teenage-children's articulation of the rich meanings present in the embodied nature of place-based outdoor nature learning in their own lives.

Billy and Ben's Experiences

Embracing the Risky Business of Teaching: A Reflection by Ben

"What do I need, Dad?" asks my son with a sleepy look in his eyes that lets me know my answers will be as quickly forgotten as they were given. I give them anyway, because planning and packing for the adventure is part of the adventure and I want him to assume the ownership for the forgotten spare shirt. The distinction between my role as teacher, father, or semi-inspired adventurist is often blurred on weekend and holiday adventures. While my son urges me to 'turn off the teacher mode', the need for each of the roles changes as the activity does. In many ways, he is the best partner in adventures – in others, he would rate among the worst. Together, for better or worse, we adventure.

In my role as Principal and Outdoor Educator in a small regional school, I assume all accountability and responsibility for the risks of the activities I plan, and facilitate experiences where others can choose to shoulder ownership and make progress. Our students mountain-bike, abseil, hike and challenge themselves on a weekly basis. It is part of our school's vision for holistic education and resilient, persistent students and I have been enthusiastically leading and shaping that vision with the knowledge of the impact it makes on me and my son. At home, *mostly* out of teacher mode, we add archery, rock-climbing, kayaking, trail-running and paddle-boarding to the activity list – but the list is always open to something new.

In my son's mind, I'm sure turning off the teacher mode means not lecturing him about the poor choice he just made – and perhaps upon reflection there is something in that. The 'lectures' seem to be mostly about choices of focus or priority during a task and/or behaviours as a reaction to a difficult task. Activity and procedural mistakes made during an activity, unless a rare dangerously unsafe decision, are observed but rarely spoken of unless I'm asked for help. I allow him to fail, repeatedly and sometimes to my quiet amusement, knowing the success will be all the greater when it is achieved. The lectures, which I think of as inspiring calls to arms, encourage ownership and focus. Hanging off a difficult route on belay, following his back wheel through a tight berm or paddling upstream to watch his progress through river strainers, I remain silent and let the activity do the teaching. It will show him when he is doing it inefficiently, or wrong, with immediate feedback. We share the ownership of the risk, he shoulders the effort to achieve success, and I assume a teaching role to reflect upon the activity at the completion of the section.

My son is a great partner, until he isn't. If I was adventuring with mates, there might be less teaching or a balance of knowledge and skill and the conversation would be more social than educational. There would be less tension in the dramatic displays of disappointment as an objective is failed – perhaps more laughs and less hope. There would be someone to share the driving and the responsibility for bringing the spare shirt! There would also be one less adventurer in the world willing to shoulder risk. I choose to champion my son's outdoor adventures and risk-taking because that is what I want for him – for every kid. The roles will soon change, and my partner will climb the crags and cruise the waterways easier than me, buoyed by the strength and energy of youth. Then I will be able to turn off the teacher mode – until he forgets the spare shirt.

Embracing the Risky Business of Learning: A Reflection by Billy

When I go with Dad adventuring, mostly I think about the physical aspects. Often it is hard work, and it is tiring physically.

But mostly adventuring is about overcoming challenges and exhaustion, and resilience.

What is going through my mind …

Are we there yet?

One more hill,

50 more strokes,

Right foot to that sloping ledge.

How much longer?

Around the corner,

Not far now,

Two inches right of centre.

I can't do it ...

... Not yet.

And then we finish what we are doing, riding down the mountain, camping through a cold night, or climbing the cliff face as high as I can go, and I know that soon I will be able to go even further, and do even more.

Jemma and Ziah's Experience

Embracing the Risky Business of Teaching: A Reflection by Jemma

I was able to capture 'risk' in socioecological learning activities in a time when the global, COVID-19 pandemic has closed schools and moved education to a 'learning from home model.' As COVID-19 required my transition from 'researcher, academic, teacher, and mum' to 'at home teacher', I was provided the opportunity to explore risky pedagogical opportunities, which practice a non-human-centric ethic of inclusion (Taylor & Guigni, 2012) into my son's educational experiences. I purposefully provided opportunities for him to build resilience and agency through scaffolded activities within his at-home educational programme through purposeful and scaffolded 'risky' explorations in rural and coastal Queensland.

To enable my son to practice autonomy and manage his own risk taking during his at-home education, I assigned a deliberate space within the 'school day' for risky socio-ecological learning activities. I captured these moments in photographs, portraying a moment in time of my teenager's life as he was building skills, character, and resilience, as an active risky socioecological learner. I thought to myself …

For a moment

There is space in the school day for exploration

For hiking and canoeing

Looking for eels and counting turtles

Discovering birds' nests, snake skins, and bush tucker …

… trying to touch the bottom of the bottomless waterhole.

There is time in the day

To learn from outside

With tools in belt and compass in hand

Gathering observations of the resilience of Australian bush animals.

Inquiring.

Stopping to hear the call of the kookaburra, and the crunch of leaves underfoot …

… to summit the top of the rock.

He is confident and capable

And able to grow in confidence and strength

Knowing he can do anything

Like build a fire, find his way home through the dense bush, and swim against a rip going to sea …

… shoot an arrow with expert precision.

I have enabled
Opportunities for him to grow
By learning through his own
socioecological experiences
Taking risks, challenging himself, trying again after initial failure …
… so he can discover how extraordinary he really is.

And all of this influences his becoming in and of the world.

Embracing the Risky Business of Learning: A Reflection by Ziah

Mum: Can you explain the emotions you feel when we do risky socioecological activities during learning from home time?

Me:

Disappointment

Frustration

Perseverance

Excitement

Joy

Tough

Anticipation

Determination

Grit

Pain

Tiring

Time consuming

Proud

Ecstatic

Fear

Fun

Exhausting

Sudden Shock

Astonishment

Mum: That is a range of emotions. Some of your words describe that you feel challenged.

Me: It is incredibly enjoyable and exciting, and it has a thrill to it. Initially there are obstacles in my path which I need to overcome. I would not be able to overcome some of these obstacles if I don't come out of my comfort zone and take some risks … challenge myself.

Mum: Do you feel safe overcoming these obstacles and taking these risks?

Me: I feel safe and confident as I am supervised by someone I trust. Some of the things I do take a long time … but in a good way. I like to see the result of things I put all this time into.

Mum: What is the most valuable skill you think you have acquired through nature-learning during your learning from home time?

Me: I think the activities that improve my perseverance, skill and overall life experiences. The skill of perseverance will help me in the future …. Perseverance is one of the most important qualities a person needs.

Conclusions: Embracing Risky Teaching and Learning

This chapter touches on our experiences as two teacher-parents as we embraced the risky business of teaching, with our two student-teenage-children as they encountered the risky business of learning. These moments captured in photographs and reflections, convey the ways our two young people were encouraged to confidently connect with their local nature-environments through activities which involved 'risky learning.' The intention was for us to capture the ways we provided scaffold risk-taking opportunities for our student-teenage-children in safe physical and supportive emotional spaces, which can support "capacity building associated with emotional and social wellbeing, and the attendant resilience and cognitive growth as well as the motivation that these attributes bring" (Wilks et al., 2020, p. 90).

We embraced outdoor nature education as a risky learning space, and synchronously enabled concepts of 'risk' and 'failure' to be used as a generative mechanisms for meaningful learning. For our two student-teenage-children, learning risk-taking in their nature-environments may empower them to take the reins of their own learning experiences and become more aware of their place and being on Earth. As young people face the myriad of challenges brought forth by the Anthropocene, it is hoped that these 'risky' outdoor activities will shape the lives of the student-teenage-children as environmentally responsible social beings, who are confident and competent in decision making and able cope with unexpected events.

References

Csikszentmihalyi, M. (2014). *Applications of flow in human development and education: The collected works of Mihaly Csikszentmihalyi*. Springer. https://doi.org/10.1007/978-94-017-9094-9

Oswald, T., Rumbold, A., Kedzior, S., & Moore, V. (2020). Psychological impacts of "screen time" and "green time" for children and adolescents: A systematic scoping review. *PloS One*, *15*(9), e0237725. https://doi.org/10.1371/journal.pone.0237725

Taylor, A., & Giugni, M. (2012). Common worlds: Reconceptualising inclusion in early childhood communities. *Contemporary Issues in Early Childhood*, *13*(2), 108–119. https://doi.org/10.2304/ciec.2012.13.2.108

Wattchow, B., & Higgins, P. (2014). Through outdoor education: A sense of place on Scotland's River Spey. In B. Wattchow, R. Jeans, L. Alfrey, T. Brown, A.

Cutter-Mackenzie, & J. O'Connor (Eds.), *The socioecological educator: A 21st century renewal of physical, health, environment and outdoor education* (pp. 173–187). Springer.

Wilks, J., Turner, A., & Shipway, B. (2020). The risky socioecological learner. In A. Cutter-Mackenzie-Knowels, A. Lasczik, J. Wilks, M. Logan, A. Turner, & W. Boyd (Eds.), *Touchstones for deterritorialzing socioecological learning.* Palgrave Macmillan.

CHAPTER 5

Vortex(t)

The Becoming of the Socioecological Learner-Teacher-Researcher

William Boyd, Marie-Laurence Paquette, Shae Brown, Euan Boyd and Adrienne Piscopo

Abstract

This chapter is an experiment. Five authors, one who wrote the scholarly article (Boyd, 2020) inspiring this chapter, and four newly introduced to it. The one and the four inhabit an interstitial space (Bhabha, 1994), a place of negotiated meaning. An iterative exchange – a telling and retelling of the story of the original article – creates new insights, new meanings and new expressions. In the external and physical reality of the discussion, twirling winds synchronize with spoken words. Through a dialogic review of structures – structures of discourse generativity, within the text, of writing together – we question linearity of time and events, and the concept of vortex emerges. The fundamental matter in hand remains: what might the learner look like in a socioecological world?

Keywords

vortex/vortex(t) – socioecological learner – posthuman – Anthropocene – common worlds – graphic story

• • •

In the original scholarly chapter, the socioecological learner was posited as playing a

> significant, unbounded role, with a responsibility to engage the world on their own terms, to be a shaper of learning, a filterer of content, a bringer of ideas, preferences, interests, value positions, emotional concerns and viewpoints to the learning situation, an experiencer of the world, embodying in-the-moment relationships between themselves, their world, peers, teachers, subject matter, task, learning outcomes, a

DOI:10.1163/9789004507838_006

> solver of real problems and a member of the global – in the true sense – and Anthropocene community: to be a seamless learner-teacher-researcher. (Boyd, 2020, p. 132)

This chapter explores ideas (Boyd, 2020) of a world where learning is unbounded, where the learner and the teacher are not 'one' – at once they are both their own person and integrated into a vortex of common learning and knowing. The paradox of individuation and connection and the tension it creates is foundational within the generative dynamics of learning and the patterns of that generativity generally, in a world where binaries are eschewed, where challenges founded on the past and present are considered, cracks in the system noted, and opportunities for emergence flagged. Matters of power and authority, knowledge and expertise, and relationships and control are explored. What might this look like in a socioecological world? What must change to be able to take full account of the past, in a way that honours a complex present and inclusive future. Is this even possible? Language shifts.

We authors play with the inherent tensions of being human in considering a posthuman world, being modern in a postmodern world. We walk and we sketch, visually, through the text, building from and towards the premise that a socioecological learner will be a merged learner-teacher-researcher, engaged in a transactional education, influenced by turbulences and twists. By vortex(t).

We were given the challenge to invent a creative version of the previous chapter. The original title was long and sensible, referencing a key influence on our thinking: "It is not a question of either/or, but of 'and... and'": The socioecological learner as learner-teacher-researcher. But as we talk, we become conscious of the eddies, of ideas floating in and out, of waves, of the wind in the trees, the wind in our minds … vortices emanating from the original text, sidelines, insights. Our text becomes. Becomes Vortex(t). We are learning. Slowly becoming the socioecological learner-teacher-researcher of the title.

We were invited to a beautiful place. We were asked to think, to talk, to create. And we were invited to walk through our own words, our own lines, our own beautiful vortext. And as we lead ourselves through poetry, images, overhead instructions, our minds wander; hearing the wind outside, watching the sun flit across the windows, tasting possibilities.

We were asked to describe our chapter in six words. So, we describe it in eighty-three. This particular pathway to a posthuman learner-teacher-researcher is about clever things, big words: Posthumanist reassembly – decentring & convergence | teacher, learner, researcher; rehumanising learning – mutual learning | supradisciplinary | relationality, de/re-territorialisation – de-territorialising 'learner-teacher' categories | re-territorialising 'learner-teacher' categories; relearning learning. Echoes and echoes and echoes of Gilles Deleuze.

VORTEX(T)
I hope the new educator is going to be interesting to spend time with
Yeah the last one put us all to sleep...
This looks different, I wonder what this is all about?
knowledge generation
today we will be discussing the topic of knowledge generation
who wants to contribute something? a question, comment or anything?
its my understanding that...
when you look at...
if we consider the notion of...
in comparison to....
another way of describing it is ...
when reflecting upon..
however...
alternatively...
how about...
in my experience...
Ok! We've got a vortex that is our vortex/vortext happening here, lets go deeper and follow what is already flowing between and around and within us here...

But others have a say: we include what we called 'curious phrases'. Rosie Braidotti contributes, "it is not a question of either/or, but of 'and … and'" (Braidotti, 2017). Munia Khan reminds us of the learner "whose toes will teach the shore how to feel a tranquil life through the wetness of sands" (Khan, 2018). We stumble upon uncommon moments for common world insights, tripping over cracks in the system of pre-Anthropocene social constructs.

Let us tell you a story.

It is a story of connections across the world, connections across thinking and ideas. It is a story of complexity and learning. It is the story of five people trying to find shared and common meaning in an emerging world in which the need for shared and common meaning – not only just between people, but most essentially between all the elements of the planet we live on – is increasingly urgent. It is a story of a small step or two towards a future in which boundaries are, at least, less absolute than the present. A future in which categories of 'learner', 'teacher', 'researcher', 'expert' (and so on and so on and so on) merge or become meaningless. A future in which categories of 'words' and 'images' flow into equilibrium – noting, of course, that as the tensions of differences and working with them is what needs to happen; equilibrium is a kind of nothing in a complex dynamic. It means everything stops. Dynamic systems operate far from equilibrium. A future of unprivileging, of levelling. A future in which the individual ceases to dominate. A future in which humanity can truly express its humanity in a socioecological world.

Let us tell you a story of people, because it will be people who make a difference, albeit in a posthuman world.

Our first person is Rosi Braidotti. Braidotti is an eminent Italian-Australian philosopher and feminist theoretician. She writes widely about changing relationships between people, humanity and the world. Braidotti recently reflected on what she called "the urgency of the Anthropocene condition" (Braidotti, 2017). The 'Anthropocene condition', by the way, refers to the current geological period. This is a period we now understand to operate, unlike any time in the world's history, under the increasing and, importantly, deleterious, influence of humanity. In considering how people might respond less deleteriously to the world, Braidotti suggests there is an urgent need for "qualitatively new discourses" – her words – in how we think about world and our place in it.

Our second person is another eminent philosopher and critical theorist, the English Indian Homi Bhabha. In 1994, he published a wonderful book entitled *The Location of Culture*. One of us, Bill, is old enough to have been around when the book came out. Amongst the riches between the book's distinctive blue covers, the idea of 'interstitial space' or 'interstices' stuck with Bill. Interstitial space – as Bill understood it – is the place or space *between* people and cultures. It is the place where meaning and identity is negotiated.

At the risk of sounding like just another scholarly article, let us indulge in a quote from Homi Bhabha. "The interstices", he informed us, are "the overlap and displacement of domains of difference – that the intersubjective and collective experiences of nationness, community interest, or cultural value are negotiated". Grand words, we will admit. What do they mean? Bill imagined the interstitial space as a mirrored honeycomb, sitting between people or peoples. But in the re-telling, together we imagine the interstitial space as a vortex, swirling between people and peoples and places. It is a multi-dimensional space where ideas are transferred, forever reflecting, changing, growing. My understanding of you is as much a function of your understanding of me as it is of my previous understanding of you … we might be wrong, but the idea of a shared between-place in which new ideas are generated has unmistakably formed between us with him since those heady *Location of Culture* days.

So … what has this little introduction to two giant and global philosophers have to do with this chapter? In short, they provide the chapter a reason-for-being. We will try to grow and be with this interstitial space to generate a qualitatively new discourse. Grand claim? Maybe. But given the urgency of the Anthropocene, worth a try.

How will we go about this? The experiment is deceptively simple.

One of us – Bill, close to the end of a career as a scholar – is the author of the original chapter in the big scholarly book. The short version of the chapter is that, when all is said and done, the socio-ecological learner is a real possibility. The big scholarly book's big scholarly title validates this claim of bigness and scholarliness: *Touchstones for Deterritorializing Socioecological Learning: The Anthropocene, Posthumanism and Commonworlds as Creative Milieux*. Bill is the one who knows the chapter inside out, having drafted it from his own experience and scholarship. Others of us – Mahi and Shae are just starting out as a scholars – had nothing to do with the chapter until we buddied up for the writing here. During our early discussions, we were introduced to Nick Sousanis, the graphic novelist whose Columbia University doctoral thesis, *Unflattening*, inspired us to expand our communication horizons (Sousanis, 2015). Enter our fourth and fifth authors, Euan Boyd and Adrienne Piscopo. They are the two halves of The Bewitching Moon, artists from the posthuman, more-than-human tradition. Their explorations of the weird and wonderful, of their abys-dweller characters, of patterns, circles and chakras as elemental communication, and of hybridities and liminalities, and most recently vortical voids, capture futures in the present. They brought their own language, a visual language – at times representational, at times abstract – but always capable of generating tension against the written language of the text. They run parallel to the text: cross referencing is irrelevant here. Despite the postmodern and posthuman approach to their art, our collective adoption of a style of overlaying and mashing up is a visual art

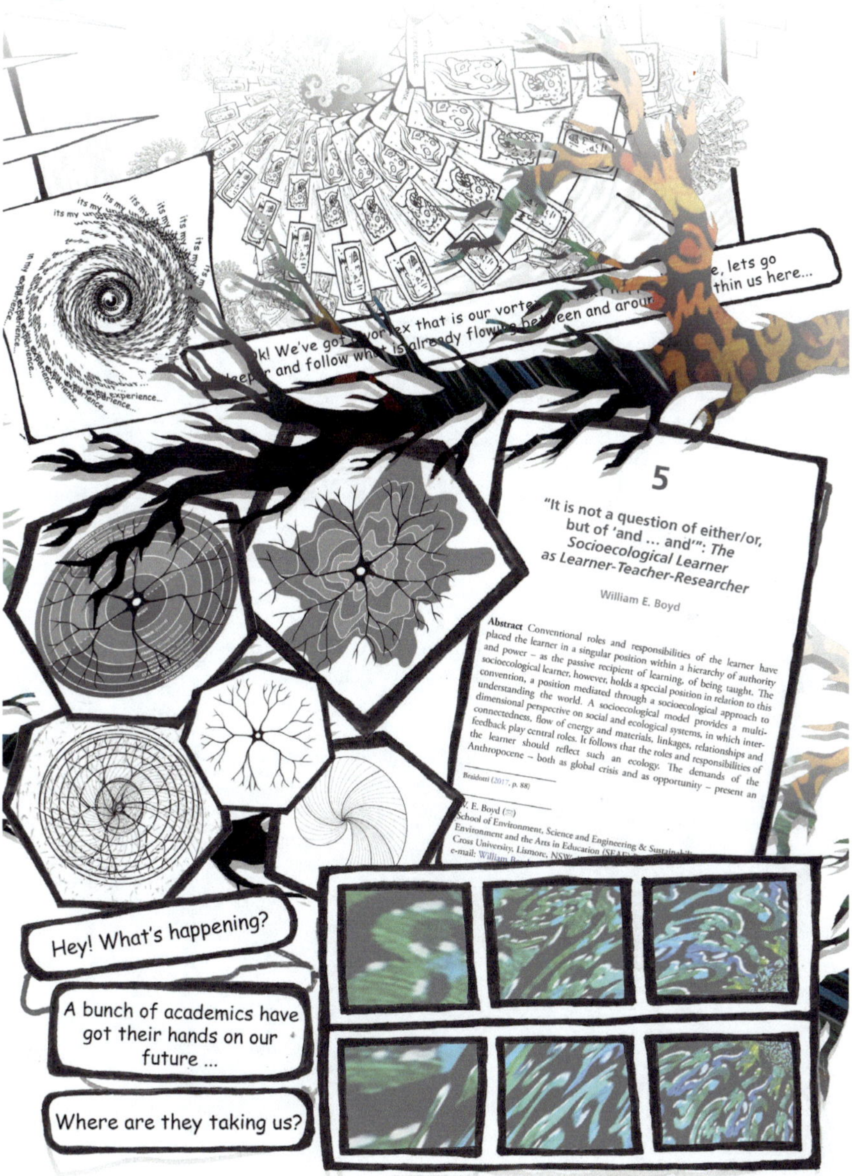
k! We've got
that is our vorte
e, lets go
r and follow wh
already flow
between and arour
thin us here...
5
"It is not a question of either/or, but of 'and ... and'": The Socioecological Learner as Learner-Teacher-Researcher
William E. Boyd
Abstract Conventional roles and responsibilities of the learner have placed the learner in a singular position within a hierarchy of authority and power – as the passive recipient of learning, of being taught. The socioecological learner, however, holds a special position in relation to this convention, a position mediated through a socioecological approach to understanding the world. A socioecological model provides a multi-dimensional perspective on social and ecological systems, in which inter-connectedness, flow of energy and materials, linkages, relationships and feedback play central roles. It follows that the roles and responsibilities of the learner should reflect such an ecology. The demands of the Anthropocene – both as global crisis and as opportunity – present an
Braidotti (2017, p. 88)
E. Boyd
School of Environment, Science and Engineering
Environment and the Arts in Education
Cross University, Lismore, NSW
e-mail:
Hey! What's happening?
A bunch of academics have got their hands on our future ...
Where are they taking us?

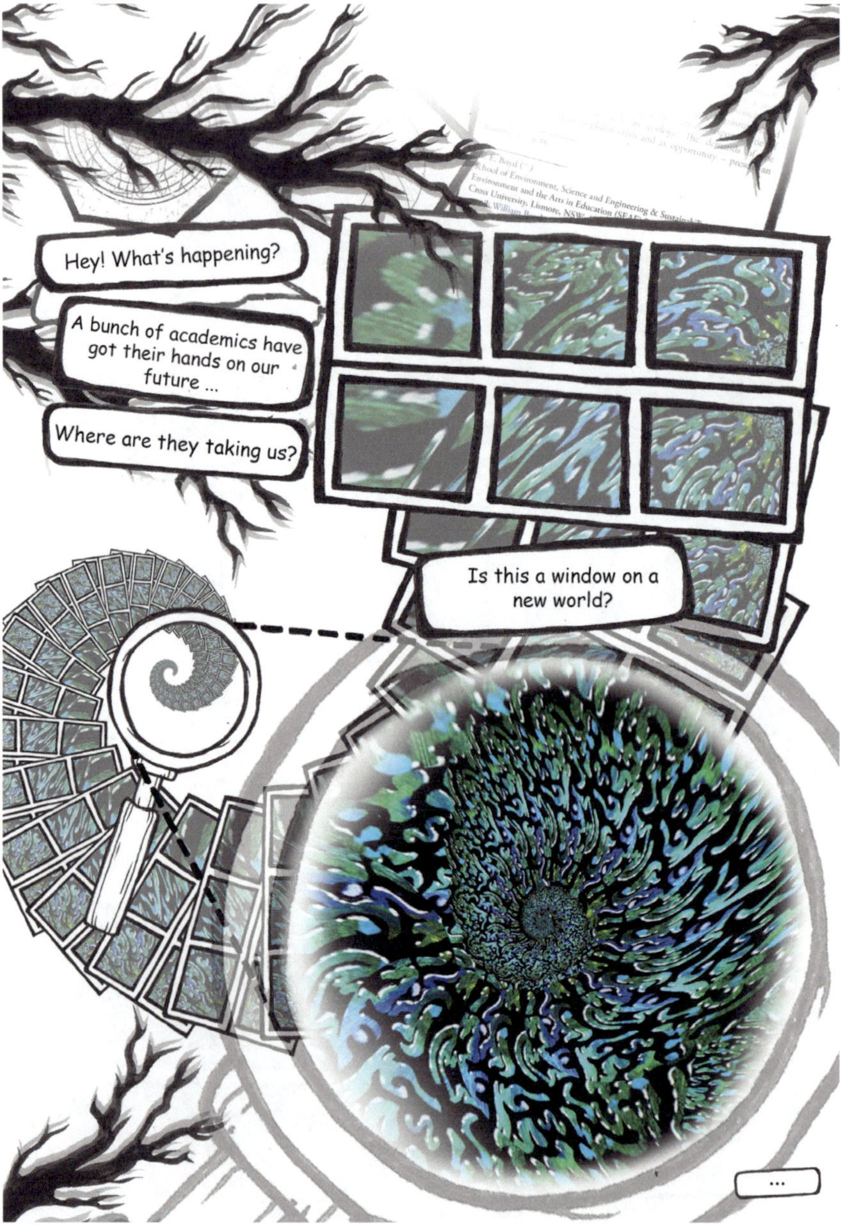
Hey! What's happening?
A bunch of academics have got their hands on our future ...
Where are they taking us?
Is this a window on a new world?
...

form and process with a long history. While we are inspired by the arts-based methodology a/r/tography, introduced by Irwin (Irwin & de Cosson, 2004) and seen in Sousanis's work, we are also inspired by the iterative process by which Sousanis engages content and graphics (Sousanis, 2020).

This new author-partnership is the experiment. In it, we all sit around and within the interstitial space. We exchange understandings. We write and we draw, reinterpreting each time, back and forth, back and forth. And as we do, meanings change, deepen, reprioritise. Insights emerge, cherished ideas fade. New linkages become evident. And, excitingly, the language changes. Doors open for new meanings, new expressions. The language of the scholarly article gives way to a broader language of the world. And while we still inhabit the interstitial space, is it possible, just vaguely possible, that that for each of us a new discourse is emerging? Maybe even a qualitatively new discourse? While we remain conscious of our interstitial positions, we can only leave it to the world to decide if newness has been achieved. In the meantime, we invite you, the reader, to walk through this experiment, through different languages, letters and forms.

Prepare yourself to enter a new path. One that goes forward and circular, one that goes sideways, and up, and down. Welcome to the vortex(t), a creation. Part graphic novel, part prose-like, born as a result of five minds, on a quest for a learner-researcher-teacher, an entanglement made available through a post-humanist glimpse. The experiment focuses on questioning and answering the authority of yesterday by embracing the turbulence of roles while surrendering to supradisciplinarity.

This piece is a storytelling of footpath, where the walk makes the talk, alongside the wobbling line of linearity, of history, of past-present-future. Prepare yourself for a convergence around a new milieu, an axis that allows for a de-centring of the status quo. We attempt to explore beyond the boxes, the silos of knowledge that have characterised the Anthropocene to this day. Vortex(t) is like a curtain opening on a vision. A door slightly open, allowing the reader to hear the echo of a brainstorm, again, turbulences emerging and re-arranging themselves under a different perspective, on a journey revealing a new possibility for the socio-ecological learner.

Vortices in their physical forms are, we are told by those who know such things (Ma et al., 2012), found in the air, in water, in fluids, in smoke and in space. They are the result of a combination of factors such as pressure, tension, obstacles, winds, angles, viscosity, flow and several more. Forming themselves around a vertical axis, they stretch the stillness of the surface to a three-dimensional perspective, while natural laws such as the Coriolis force dictate the rotation's way. A vortex is a physicality of the pulsations of the world, of its roundness, cyclicity and turbulences. In physical sciences, cracks,

… and so, dear vortex travellers, we come to a new beginning …
a new dynamic in the teaching-learning-researching experience … where we can acknowledge agency and relationships …
engage the flows and tensions of diverse energies and perspectives … thrive on mutually generative learning …
…

blockages, twists, ruptures are investigated to better comprehend the mechanisms of motion that disturb events of stationary equilibrium of a rotating and gravitational planet Earth.

The vortex reminds us that all systems of matter operate in dynamic movement at all times and maintain existence and generativity through the movement itself.

In light of the complexity of physical structures such a vortices, we question the constancy of their existence. One could argue that seeking a state of equilibrium used to be a constant, a common goal. In opposition to this commonly held goal, breaking equilibrium as a constant would represent another side of a duality. We put forward the idea that, perhaps, the momentum between those binaries, the vortex, is the temporary balance between a range of different and moving forces. Stillness is a momentary betweenness that exists mostly in mediation. Yet, even then, the body is in continual dynamic movement. The spin in action, the movement itself, between turbulences and motionlessness, is the new equilibrium. This idea serves as a metaphor for the chaos and order as continual dynamics encountered in life as a whole, more particularly in human interactions and in the reality of education. Is managing to be generative among the increasing dynamics and turbulence required for being a sociological learner?

Learning and knowledge generation are described in Bill's original chapter as needing to reflect the complex ecology of the interconnected world we are all in and of, with and as; the Industrial revolution model still operating in schools is way out of date. This is a new millennium. We are in a new era, or at least in transition between eras – the Anthropocene and what may come.

Life is complex. Life is fluid. And life requires capacity for a multidimensional way of learning. A way that includes so much more information than the old transfer models of fixed curriculum and a tolerance for change and turbulence. A way that embraces the breaking down of the boundaries of learner-teacher-researcher, and the boundaries of knower and known in a posthuman sensibility.

The compendium in which this chapter resides values the notion of flat ontology as an alternative to the hierarchical vertical ontology with humans at the top of a ladder of importance, and a hierarchy between humans as well. We seek an alternative. An alternative to open spaces of the possible within education. An alternative to disturb fixed linear power. An alternative to include the wide range of ebbs, flows and forces within learning. The myriad of facets of the socio-ecological learner-teacher-researcher, the process and content, the entities and materialities, the agency of spaces, buildings, the environment: all as an entirety (Cutter-Mackenzie et al., 2020). Discourse exists within, and is inseparable, from all places and material arrangements, with generativity in the discursive-materiality of all matter and phenomena described through

Barad's consideration of quantum physics (Barad, 2007). So, therefore, we are not sure that the ontological flatness seen in the work of Deleuze and Guattari (1978/2004) is sufficient, not sure it opens and widens the rigid linearity of the vertical hierarchy enough, and … there is more – more dimensions in the multidimensionality of the socio-ecological learning 'space of the possible' (Sumara & Davis, 1997). Flatness does not move enough to encompass the seething multidimensionality of the entangled interweaving and intertwingling of the posthuman world. And so, the ontological flatness seen in the work of Deleuze and Guattari is not enough, and we are not sure it opens and widens the rigid linearity of the vertical hierarchy enough.

Yes, at this stage we are not sure: but we are certain of the need for further exploration. We do feel, however, that there is more – more dimensions in the multidimensionality of the socio-ecological learning 'space of the possible'. We do not have, however, the luxury of time that Deleuze and Guattari have had to explore and articulate in their recovery of the flat ontology. It needs further interrogation, and interrogation that must surely follow our preliminary explorations in this chapter.

In opening up the learning experience to the fluidity of the socio-ecological learning approach, there is also the need to acknowledge that, while flows of power and agency can be distributed and can be inclusive, the flows and dynamics are not always identical. There are salient arrangements and re-arrangements of dynamics, in complex patterns of relationship and co-mutuality (Brown, 2019). And so, we look to relationship with patterns to consider how dynamic ecological forms can assist people to engage generatively with complexity and fluidity. Even the most egalitarian and inclusive socio-ecological situations require agreement of form and process for relating and generating knowledge. Shae's recent work on patterns, for example, is a useful approach to engaging with complex phenomena such as education and helps us understand that many Indigenous peoples have used patterns as metaphor and co-generative practice in relationship with phenomena (Brown, 2019). Her multidimensional ecological flow-form approach to complexity patterning shows the usefulness of ecological forms in approaches to learning and energises the entangled engagement with patterns.

In this chapter, we use a vortex pattern – a vortex form – as a metaphor and method for engaging in knowledge building across boundaries. It is a way of engaging learners with full acknowledgement of agency and relationship within the dynamics of the teaching-learning-researching experience. In a vortex form, interrelatedness and difference are both needed to create the powerful form of a vortex. A form that spins with the tensions of forces from more than one direction, generating a two-dimensional surface spin, until a 'critical spin' generates the third dimension of depth.

Dynamic movement is perpetual and inevitable, in relationship, in life and in learning. Engaging with the flows and tensions of diverse energies and perspectives can enable the socio-ecological learner-teacher-researcher to stay with the dynamics – the vortex(t) – of mutually generative learning.

References

Barad, K. (2007). *Meeting the universe halfway: Quantum physics and the entanglement of matter and meaning*. Duke University Press.

Bhabha, H. K. (1994). *The location of culture*. Routledge. doi:10.4324/9780203820551

Boyd, W. E. (2020). "It is not a question of either/or, but of 'and … and'": The socioecological learner as learner-teacher-researcher. In A. Cutter-Mackenzie, A. Lasczik, J. Wilks, M. R. Logan, A. Turner, & W. Boyd (Eds.), *Touchstones for deterritorializing socioecological learning: The Anthropocene, posthumanism and common worlds as creative milieux*. Palgrave Macmillan. doi:10.1007/978-3-030-12212-6

Braidotti, R. (2017). Critical posthuman knowledges. *South Atlantic Quarterly, 116*(1), 83–96. doi:10.1215/00382876-3749337

Brown, S. (2019). A patterning approach to complexity thinking and understanding for students: A case study. *Northeast Journal of Complex Systems (NEJCS), 1*(1), 6.

Cutter-Mackenzie, A., Lasczik, A., Wilks, J., Logan, M. R., Turner, A., & Boyd, W. (Eds.). (2020). *Touchstones for deterritorializing socioecological learning: The Anthropocene, posthumanism and common worlds as creative milieux*. Palgrave Macmillan. doi:10.1007/978-3-030-12212-6

Deleuze, G., & Guattari, F. (2004). *A thousand plateaus: Capitalism and schizophrenia*. University of Minnesota Press. (Original work published 1980)

Irwin, R., & de Cosson, A. (2004). *A/r/tography: Rendering self through arts-based living inquiry*. Pacific Educational Press.

Khan, M. (2018). *Goodreads*. https://www.goodreads.com/quotes/7883514-let-my-toes-teach-the-shore-how-to-feel-a

Ma, Y., Kafatos, M., & Davidson, N. E. (2012). Surface pressure profiles, vortex structure and initialization for hurricane prediction. Part I: Analysis of observed and synthetic structures. *Meteorology and Atmospheric Physics, 117*(1–2), 5–23. doi:10.1007/s00703-012-0190-z

Sousanis, N. (2015). *Unflattening*. Harvard University Press.

Sousanis, N. (2020). *Sketching entropy: How an idea becomes a comic page*. http://spinweaveandcut.com/sketching-entropy/

Sumara, D. J., & Davis, B. (1997). Enlarging the space of the possible: Complexity, complicity, and action-research practices. *Counterpoints, 67*, 299–312.

Vikulin, A. V., Ivanchin, A. G., & Tveritinova, T. Y. (2011). Moment vortex geodynamics. *Moscow University Geology Bulletin, 66*(1), 29–36. doi:10.3103/s014587521101008x

CHAPTER 6

Big (Hi)Story

Experimenting with Deep-Time

Marilyn Ahearn and Teresa Carapeto

Abstract

This chapter explores the significance of the deep-time story of the universe to environmental education, reimagining the place of socioecological learning within the contexts of the evolving deep-time scientific story and the Anthropocene. We use the concept of 'journey' as the metaphor to transcend 'in-between' entanglements (Barad, 2007, 2010) of place/deep-time, adding richer layers of intuitive understandings to the existing scientific evidence on this subject. We incorporate arts-based forms through imagery, photography, art, prose, poetic dialogue and reflective discourse to forge broader perspectives, new connections and understandings of interdependence within the increasing unfoldings of our complex universe. The 13.8-billion-year Big History framework is reviewed through three pivotal signposts in time. The interconnected signposts traverse the flaring forth of the universe and its boundless possibilities, continuing its projectory through the emergence of elements as building blocks for non-living matter, nature, creatures, humans and the ticking clock of future possibilities for everyThing and everyOne. Our hope is that our intuitive interpretations of the scientific universe story resonate with socioecological learning, thus empowering hope and agency, in encompassing all aspects of the environment, the 'non-human', the 'human' and the 'more-than-human'.

Keywords

Big History – socioecological learning – Anthropocene – deep time – arts-based

Orientation

> Who in the world am I? Ah, that's the great puzzle! (Lewis Carroll)

Socioecological learning embraces the environment, economics, society, culture and well-being perspectives, relying on the entanglements of

DOI:10.1163/9789004507838_007

transdisciplinary learning that "looks not only across and between disciplines but also beyond them" (Burford et al., 2013). The transdisciplinary contributions offered in the following pages are to be viewed through the lenses of deep-time (Delgardo, 2014; Irvine, 2014) and arts-based research (Irwin, 2013; Cutter-Mackenzie-Knowles et al., 2020).

Ingold's explanation of knots and entanglements (2010, 2015) lend themselves to the task we set ourselves, of creatively packing and journeying in spacetime mattering. Malone explains this term as "expanding the range of multiple ways of being, both in [one place] and in the world at large" (2015, p. 197). This visual essay navigates an artful representation of Big History, an entangled 13.8 billion year deep-time universe story. We entangle with the evidence from a deep-time orientation to create critical images that enhance our "theoretical dispositions regarding the object/subject under study [making it] a critical text in its own right" (Lasczik Cutcher, 2018, p. 95). We collaboratively and creatively engage through the lens of a/r/tography, its embodied practice (Rousell & Cutcher, 2014: Rousell et al., 2020) and slow scholarship (Lasczik Cutcher & Irwin, 2017).

In resonating with fiction, we freed ourselves to re-imagine an interrelated and knotted world of future possibilities for the 'more than human' (Malone, 2015). Lazlo (2018) describes "a path to connect life … with our more-than-human world, and with past and future generations of all beings in service of thriving futures" (p. 182). Likewise, directions on our compass in this work point towards a journey encompassing space/deeptime interconnectedness with everyThing and everyOne.

Our collaborative writing journey began at a writers' retreat in 2019 where we wandered through the natural environment, sharing our respective expertise and interests from arts-based and deep-time research perspectives. In this setting we cooperatively sought and developed pivotal signposts for our entangled journeying though this chapter, with vignettes from Lewis Carroll's *Alice in Wonderland* and *Through the Looking Glass* (1872, 1886) permeating our imagination and informing directions for our exploration. Although we acknowledge there are differing allegorical interpretations of Alice in Wonderland (Brown, 2005; Irwin & Davis, 2009), for the purposes of this chapter we concentrated on our own childhood memories of the story and allowed the echo of Alice's words to lead us creatively towards environmental signposts.

The dream-child moving through a land
Of wonders wild and new …

Thus grew the tale of Wonderland:
Thus slowly, one by one,
Its quaint events were hammered out.[1]

Particular scenes from Alice's journeys down the rabbit hole and through the looking glass, resonated with us through the intertwined pivotal signposts of deep-time, engaging the Big History framework to explore the wonders of our universe. In this chapter we engage metaphorically with echoes of Alice and her Wonderland, not to imitate her unique journey, but rather to inspire, as we set out on our own exploration of a deep-time universe wonderland.

We too, searching,
for a land of wonders ...

Discover echoes of Alice's journey encouraging us on ...

We too, dreaming,
swiftly gliding

Sensing the brILLIAnce

of the immensity of stars
with our untold Wonderland stories yet to be uncovered

We too, finding,
Images of deep-time fLASh before us

EnTaNgLeD ______________ dazzling our eyes!

Time Space
Origin
..Stories
Deep Time Story
Universe
Wonderland
Time & Space

Our journey moves through the wonderland of our 'common world' (Latour, 2014; Taylor, 2017), 13.8 billion-year old universe. To explain, we journey to the beginning of deep-time as we know it (Ahearn, 2019; Delgado, 2014; Irvine, 2014), in order to discover the wonderland of Big History (Big History Project, 2018; Christian, 2011, 2017). As we fall down the rabbit hole, like Alice we journey into the deep-time wonderland of the universe that opens boundless joint learning possibilities and wonders for education, crossing multiple disciplinary boundaries (Gillis et al., 2017; Klein, 2008; UNESCO, 1997).

In resonating with Alice's journey, we also embark on an imaginative world of possibilities, encouraging reflection and expansion on previous writing of post-anthropocentric imaginaries of the socioecological learner in the deep-time story offered by Big History (Ahearn et al., 2020). Wonderland lies before us as we embrace transient thinking and possibilities for transforming interrelationships with common worlds. We endeavour to form new connections through our own musings through echoes of Wonderland.

As we gaze through the interactive lens of the common worlds of the universe story where Big History offers 'wonders wild and new', past/present/future imaginings are entangled. Big History underpins our reflections with its emphasis on an interconnected and coherent origin story that seeks to explain the past and present and to pose possibilities for the future. It empowers learners to investigate differing scales of space and time, and to reflect on origin stories that have emerged throughout human history. The process of critical inquiry inspires learners to probe into scientific and historical discoveries that merge and interweave a modern, scientific origin story (Christian, 2011; Big History Project, 2020a, 2020b).

An invitation to journey through Deep-time …

A snapshot in time
within the limitless MACRO COSMOS:
the feet of trees
in the deep-time of the ancient Earth.

Travelling through space/deeptime we discover the story unfolding, beginning with everything, introducing the pathway of Life, evolving into pre-human, human and post-human.

R
E
M
B
E
R
I
N
G
S ...

Unlike Alice, our journey does not end with her exclamation,

'*Oh, I've had such a curious dream!*'

Rather, our universe journey
opens us up to the posthuman
with boundless opportunities
to contemplate the future
for transformative thinking.

Slowly ⇒ *pivotal signposts* ⇒ *eMERGE ...*

1. *The universe flares forth: everyThing*
2. *Pathways to life, humans, anthropocentrism: everyOne*
3. *Future possibilities: everyThing and everyOne!*

Signpost One – The Universe Flares Forth: EveryThing

We will take the King's advice to 'Begin at the beginning' and so we heed Alice's adventurous beginnings to her adventure:

> *The rabbit-hole went straight on like a tunnel for some way, and then dipped suddenly down, so suddenly that Alice had not a moment to think about stopping herself before she found herself falling down what seemed to be a very deep well.*[2]

Universe flares forth,

with boundless possibilities!

Dying stars – elements! Solar-systems building blocks!

everyThing

Boundless possibilities,
A continuing projectory
through the emergence of elements

as building **blocks** *of our universe,*

... the essence of ***EVERYTHING*** *and* ***EVERYONE!***

any
road…

We begin our adventure in a beautiful garden
… touched by humans,
… relationships emerge -
Common worlds of existence

Then, as if in a dream – a holographic image of a cat

appears in mid-air …

Dare I say – the cat speaks!

if you don't know where you are going, any road will get you there.[3]

The cat stares ... we travel on,
Like eagle hawks in synchronicity
Entangled in a myriad of galaxies – an infinite universe

As Alice became immersed in her Wonderland she realised Dinah her cat would miss her but there were too many unknown adventures lying before her. Her limited conception of the world was unravelling:

I know who I was when I got up this morning, but I think I must have been changed several times since then.[4]

We travel in parallel with Alice's sensations, in that our first signpost deepened our immersion into a vast, universe origin story to which we all belong, a knotting of the more than human – the story of a Big History of common worlds.

Signpost Two
Now beckons us onward!

As we attempt to follow our second signpost, we realise there are many roads on our map, leaving us with a dilemma – which one to take? We look to echoes of Alice's words for advice on our next move:

There were doors all round the hall, but they were all locked; ... trying every door, she walked sadly down the middle, wondering how she was ever to get out.

Suddenly she came upon a little table ... a tiny golden key ... she tried the little golden key in the lock ... it fitted!

Alice had begun to think that very few things indeed were really impossible.[5]

Alice's discovery of the right key for her adventure leads us on the road to discover the emergence of our own place in space – namely the solar system, the Earth and the emergence of life (Christian, 2018; Collins et al., 2013).

Signpost Two – Pathways to Life, Humans, Anthropocentrism: EveryOne

As we continue our investigation of the universe story, we too begin to think that very few things are really impossible. It becomes increasingly clear that understanding the complexity of our universe transcends to a deeper understanding of the interconnection of all that is non-human, human and more than human (Panelli, 2010) – whole systems thinking (Laszlo & Krippner, 1998; Leiserowitz & Fernandez, 2008; Sterling, 2003, 2010)!

Universe blooms forth
into oceans, forests!
Fish, birds, insects, mammals
complex entanglement!
Human cultures' impact
Universal Entanglements …

e
L
e
M e
N t

Rememberings of a snapshot in time

within the limitless macro cosmos.

A classic urn from yesteryear,

Gently placed upon a pier.

Greening Nature flowing within.

Interweaving the continuing story –

The Big Bang – helium, hydrogen,

Elements emerge

Solar systems, Planets, Earth

Environments emerge, life!

Rememberings of a snapshot in time …

A feeling of peace,
coupled with a sensation of dense stillness.

Utter quietness holds us
suspended infinitely in time.

Lingering in that moment,
listening to our beating hearts.
Heavy. Wide. Bursting.

Falling
down,
down,
down
Alice's rabbit hole.

A **MAGNIFICENT** sight greets our eyes!

Earth (by Kevin M. Gill, Creative Commons, https://commons.wikimedia.org/wiki/File:Earth_(16531230438).jpg)

Then from a distance, we hear a voice from another time gently whispering…

> Suddenly, from behind the rim of the moon, in long, slow-motion moments of immense majesty, there emerges a sparkling blue and white jewel, a light, delicate sky-blue sphere laced with slowly swirling veils of white, rising gradually like a small pearl in a thick sea of black mystery. It takes more than a moment to fully realise this is Earth … home.[6]

We learn from Alice's dilemmas as she met characters issuing confusing statements, including the Queen's utterance, *It's a poor sort of memory that only works backwards*. During our travels through deep-time we arrive at our own current dilemma: the demands that anthropocentrism[7] places on our future (Bonnett, 2015; Gough, 2015).

As we attempt to locate Signpost Three in this deep-time entanglement, it would be wise to heed Humpty Dumpty's advice to Alice and consider some options:

> *It would be just as well if you'd mention what you mean to do next, as I suppose you don't mean to stop here all the rest of your life.*[8]

Which way now?

Where is our third signpost?

… What are our options?

… Are we heeding the call for the posthuman?

… *Sustainability*?

An Angel sleeps amongst it all – frozen in time

For us though,
deep-time entangles,

Calling us on to reconnect in our common worlds

Signpost Three beckons us on!

trois
trois
trois

Signpost Three – Future Possibilities

Posthumanism: EveryThing and EveryOne

When we regard our future, are there further words of wisdom we can take from Alice's learning?

> Alice asked, *Would you tell me, please, which way I ought to go from here?*
> *That depends a good deal on where you want to get to,* said the Cat.[9]

The distant words of the Cheshire Cat
echo around us,
reminding us
to choose **our own road** for **our entangled story**.

How does 13.8 billion years

Morph into our future story line?

DEEP-TIME … so many stories!

... which Story?

... EveryThing and EveryOne!

The Cheshire Cat's words of wisdom echo in our Wonderland travels. If humans are to regain common grounding,[10] a wider worldview[11] for everyOne and everyThing, then an integrated understanding of the significance of the interweaving of deep-time in the universe story is needed. It is crucial in dealing with unknown futures of greater complexity that our universe's time is not viewed merely as lineal; rather it intertwines a deeper sense of an interconnecting framework of our place, embracing past, present and future.

As Big History is based on interdisciplinary, critical inquiry and the common grounding of deep-time, the unfolding, intertwined story calls to be updated as new evidence is discovered in the depths of wisdom encompassing past, present and future. Expert thinking from many academic disciplines continues to unfold an evidence-based coherent universe story. A wider, whole-system, posthuman understanding interweaves the many possibilities for future new learning and innovation.

Take children out to the stars
show them Wonder
Origin of the Universe
Origin of life
This Wonderful reality
Available to children
Through entanglements with Deep-Time!

Nature ... Evolution ... Humanity

Transdisciplinary learning
Impacts on
Our entangled storyline

Co-becoming[12] *... EveryThing* ***and*** *EveryOne!*

Nature … Evolution … Humanity

… interconnectedness
… interrelationships
… interdependence
…interdisciplinary

Common worlds … Future Agency and Hope!

H
H
H
Zn
C
N
Na
Rh
Sc
H
Ba
Fr
Ac
Rf
Db
Sg
Bh
Hs
Ra
Mt
Ds
Rg
Cn
Nh
Fi

[Alice would] *in the after-time, be herself a grown woman … and how she would gather about her other little children, and make their eyes bright and eager with many a strange tale, perhaps even with the dream of Wonderland of long-ago.*[13]

As we prepare to farewell echoes of Alice in her ‘after-time’, our own entangled ‘after-time’ signpost beckons us towards a complex and interwoven, deep-time understanding of our universal wonderland.

Our adventures now diverge, unfolding and knotting stories past and present, projecting into the future, sharing wisdom for the sake of

everyOne **and** everyThing!

Breathing in the aroma of the earth,
that fresh moist compost.

Leaves of green brighten our vision,
In shades non-existent to human-centred reality.

The soil, rich in vitality.
Seeping through our toes,
lovingly supporting the soles
of our feet.

We have landed softly
on a planet we call Home.

Acknowledging entanglements of deep-time *and* space.

Epilogue Farewell to Alice: Our journeys digress

The beginning: seeing with OUR worldview
On a discovery to our WIDER WORLDVIEW
Of places and times unimaginable
Through the lens of 13.8 billion years of Big History.

Reflecting on past present, and future – Deep-time!
Encompassing human and nonhuman,
Embracing transdisciplinary learning,
Interconnectedness of space and time

Resilience to revisit the adventures
From our place in deep-time!
Ongoing critical analysis – Socioecological learning
Paradigm shifts – inform, transform perception
to ...

Non-human, human, more than human –

Common worlds

EveryOne and EveryThing

Notes

1 Carroll (1872, 1886).
2 Carroll (1886, chapter 7).
3 Carroll (1886).
4 Carroll (1886, chapter 5).
5 Carroll (1886, prologue).
6 U.S Astronaut Edgar Mitchell (1971, as cited in Stewart & Lynch, 2008).
7 Anthropocentrism is to place "human interests and concerns at the centre of the relationship between people and the environment" (Ashley, 2006, p. 89).
8 Carroll (1872, chapter 6).
9 Carroll (1872, chapter 6).
10 See Earth Charter Commission (2000); Taylor (2017).
11 See Cassell and Nelson (2010); Sterling (2003, 2011).
12 'Co-becoming … everything exists in a state of emergence and relationality … human, animal, plant, process, thing … their very being is constituted through relationships that are constantly re-generated … co-becoming to place/space (Country et al., 2016, p. 457).
13 Carroll (1886, chapter 12); Smith and Ahearn (2019).

References

Ahearn, M. (2019). *An Tairseach (threshold): An exploration of connecting the emerging scientific story of the universe to authentic Catholic primary school environmental education* [Doctor of Philosophy thesis]. Southern Cross University. https://epubs.scu.edu.au/theses/635/

Ahearn, M., Cutter-Mackenzie-Knowles, A., Shipway, B., & Boyd, W. (2020). The socioecological learner in Big History: Post-anthropocene Imageries. In A. Cutter-Mackenzie-Knowles, A. Lasczik, J. Wilks, M. Logan, A. Turner, & W. Boyd (Eds.), *Touchstones for deterritorializing socioecological learning: The Anthropocene, posthumanism and common worlds as creative milieux* (pp. 49–74). Palgrave Macmillan.

Ashley, M. (2006). Finding the right kind of awe and wonder: The metaphysical potential of religion to ground an environmental ethic. *Canadian Journal of Environmental Education, 11*(1), 88–99.

Barad, K. (2007). *Meeting the universe halfway: Quantum physics and the entanglement of matter and meaning.* Duke University Press.

Barad, K. (2010). Quantum entanglements and hauntological relations of inheritance: Dis/continuities, spacetime enfoldings, and justice-to-come. *Derrida Today, 3*(2), 240–268.

Big History Project. (2018). *Big History Project: Schools.* https://www.bighistoryproject.com/pages/schools

Big History Project. (2020a). *The Big History Project.* https://www.oerproject.com/Big-History

Big History Project. (2020b). *Unit 1: What is Big History?* https://www.oerproject.com/OER-Media/PDFs/SBH/Unit-1/Resources/U1-Unit-Guide

Bonnett, M. (2015). The powers that be: Environmental education and the transcendent. *Policy futures in Education, 13*(1), 42–56. doi:10.1177/1478210314566730

Brown, M. (2005). Making sense of nonsense: An examination of Lewis Carroll's Alice's Adventures in Wonderland and Norton Juster's The Phantom Tollbooth as allegories of children's learning. *The Looking Glass: New Perspectives on Children's Literature, 9*(1). https://www.lib.latrobe.edu.au/ojs/index.php/tlg/article/view/122/117

Carroll, L. (1865). *Alice's adventures in Wonderland.* https://en.wikisource.org/wiki/Alice%27s_Adventures_in_Wonderland_(1866)

Carroll, L. (1871). *Through the looking-glass, and what Alice found there.* https://en.wikisource.org/wiki/Through_the_Looking-Glass,_and_What_Alice_Found_There

Cassell, J., & Nelson, T. (2010). Visions lost and dreams forgotten: Environmental education, systems thinking, and possible futures in American public schools. *Teacher Education Quarterly, 37*(4), 179–197.

Christian, D. (2011). The history of our world in 18 minutes. *TED = ideas worth spreading.* http://www.ted.com/talks/david_christian_big_history.html

Christian, D. (2017). What is Big History? *Journal of Big History, 1*(1), 4–19.

Christian, D. (2018). *Origin story: A Big History of everything*. Penguin.

Collins, D., Genet, R., & Christian, D. (2013). Crafting a new narrative to support sustainability. In W. W. Institute (Ed.), *State of the world 2013: Is sustainability still possible?* Island Press.

Country, B., Wright, S., Suchet-Pearson, S., Lloyd, K., Burarrwanga, L., Ganambarr, R., & Sweeney, J. (2016). Co-becoming Bawaka: Towards a relational understanding of place/space. *Progress in Human Geography, 40*(4), 455–475.

Cutter-Mackenzie-Knowles, A., Lasczik, A., Logan, M., Wilks, J., & Turner, A. (2020). Touchstones for deterritorializing the socioecological learner. In A. Cutter-Mackenzie-Knowles, A. Lasczik, J. Wilks, M. Logan, A. Turner, & W. Boyd (Eds.), *Touchstones for deterritorializing socioecological learning* (pp. 1–26). Palgrave Macmillan.

Delgado, C. (2013). Navigating deep-time: Landmarks for time from the big bang to the present. *Journal of Geoscience Education, 61*(1), 103–112. http://ezproxy.scu.edu.au/login?url=https://search.proquest.com/docview/1318939513?accountid=16926

Delgado, C. (2014). Collective landmarks for deep-time: A new tool for evolution education. *Journal of Biological Education, 48*(3), 133–141. doi:10.1080/00219266.2013.849280

Earth Charter Commission. (2000). *Earth charter*. http://earthcharter.org/

Gillis, D., Nelson, J., Driscoll, B., Hodgins, K., Fraser, E., & Jacobs, S. (2017). Interdisciplinary and transdisciplinary research and education in Canada: A review and suggested framework. *Collected Essays on Learning and Teaching, 10*, 203–222.

Gough, N. (2015). Undoing anthropocentrism in educational inquiry: A phildickian space odyssey. *Posthumanism and Educational Research*, 151–166.

Ingold, T. (2010). *Bringing things back to life: Creative entanglements in a world of materials*. University of Manchester. http://eprints.ncrm.ac.uk/1306/

Ingold, T. (2015). *The life of lines*. Routledge.

Irvine, R. (2014). Deep-time: An anthropological problem. *Social Anthropology, 22*(2), 157–172. doi:10.1111/1469-8676.12067

Irwin, R. L. (2013). Becoming a/r/tography. *Studies in Art Education, 54*(3), 198–215.

Irwin, R. L., Beer, R., Springgay, S., Grauer, K., Xiong, G., & Bickel, B. (2006). trans-disciplinary research. *American Journal of Preventive Medicine, 35*(2), S116–S123.

Irwin, R. L., & Springgay, S. (2017). A/r/tography as practice-based transdisciplinary research. *American Journal of Preventive Medicine, 35*(2), S116–S123.

Irwin, W., & Davis, R. B. (2009). *Alice in Wonderland and philosophy: Curiouser and curiouser* (Vol. 20). John Wiley & Sons.

Klein, J. T. (2008). Evaluation of interdisciplinary and transdisciplinary research. *American Journal of Preventive Medicine, 35*(2), S116–S123.

Lasczik Cutcher, A. (2018). Pentimento: An ethnic identity revealed, concealed, revealed. In L. Knight & A. Lasczik Cutcher (Eds.), *Arts-research-education: Connections and directions* (pp. 87–100). Springer.

Lasczik Cutcher, A., & Irwin, R. L. (2017). Walkings-through paint: A c/a/r/tography of slow scholarship. *Journal of Curriculum and Pedagogy, 14*(2), 116–124.

Laszlo, A. (2018). Leadership and systemic innovation: Socio-technical systems, ecological systems, and evolutionary systems design. *International Review of Sociology, 28*(3), 380–391. doi:10.1080/03906701.2018.1529076

Laszlo, A., & Krippner, S. (1998). Systems theories: Their origins, foundations, and development. *Advances in Psychology, 126*, 47–74.

Latour, B. (2014). Another way to compose the common world. *HAU: Journal of Ethnographic Theory, 4*(1), 301–307. http://dx.doi.org.ezproxy.scu.edu.au/10.14318/hau4.1.016

Leiserowitz, A., & Fernandez, L. (2008). Toward a new consciousness: Values to sustain human and natural communities. *Environment: Science and Policy for Sustainable Development, 50*(5), 1–65.

Malone, K., Truong, S., & Gray, T. (2017). *Reimagining sustainability in precarious times*. Singapore: Springer.

Panelli, R. (2010). More-than-human social geographies: Posthuman and other possibilities. *Progress in Human Geography, 34*(1), 79–87.

Rousell, D., & Cutcher, A. (2014). Echoes of a c/a/r/tography: Mapping the practicum experiences of pre-service visual arts teachers in the 'visual echoes project'. *Australian Art Education, 36*(2), 69.

Rousell, D., Lasczik, A., Irwin, R. L., Peisker, J., Ellis, D., & Hotko, K. (2020). Site/sight/insight: Becoming a socioecological learner through collaborative artmaking practices. In A. Cutter-Mackenzie-Knowles, A. Lasczik, J. Wilks, M. Logan, A. Turner, & W. Boyd (Eds.), *Touchstones for deterritorializing socioecological learning* (pp. 163–187). Springer.

Sterling, S. (2003). *Whole systems thinking as a basis for paradigm change in education: Explorations in the context of sustainability.* University of Bath.

Sterling, S. (2010). Learning for resilience, or the resilient learner? Towards a necessary reconciliation in a paradigm of sustainable education. *Environmental Education Research, 16*(5–6), 511–528.

Stewart, I. S., & Lynch, J. (2008). *Earth: The biography*. National Geographic Books.

Taylor, A. (2017). Romancing or re-configuring nature in the anthropocene? Towards common worlding pedagogies. In K. Malone, S. Truiong, & T. Gray (Eds.), *Reimagining sustainability in precarious times* (pp. 61–75). Springer.

UNESCO. (1997). *Educating for a sustainable future: A transdisciplinary vision for concerted action*. http://unesdoc.unesco.org/images/0011/001106/110686eo.pdf

CHAPTER 7

Sight/Site/Insight-ful Socioecological Learning Revisited

Further Collaborative Arts-Based Experimentations In-Place

Alexandra Lasczik, Adrienne Brown, Katie Hotko, David Ellis and David Rousell

Abstract

This chapter draws from Rousell, Lasczik, Irwin, Peisker, Ellis and Hotko's (2020) work on the becoming-socioecological learner through collaborative artmaking practices. Through further Artful experiments, the collective production of 'site/sight-specific' images and poetic texts are again experienced as a series of socioecological thought experiments. The touchstones of the posthuman and creative milieux of socioecological learning are further unpacked as we again seek a generative and visually critical expose, which locates the emergence of the socioecological learner as a larval subject – always becoming, always emerging, in a dynamic potentiality. The concept of the larval subject is teased out further through a distilling, and a processual engagement in further collaborative artmaking, poetry and visual essay.

Keywords

affect – c/a/r/tography – collaborative artmaking – enabling constraints – materiality site-specific artmaking – larval subject – visual essay

Openings

This chapter returns to aesthetic engagements in/with place through socioecological learning, after Rousell et al. (2020), who asserted Deleuzian concepts of the larval subject as a metonymy of emergence and becoming. The larval subject is asserted as a posthuman potential for the interactive materialisation of the socioecological learner within a biosocial ecology of sensation and

DOI:10.1163/9789004507838_008

affect. Rather than mapping as in Rousell et al.'s (2020) original work, in this chapter we lean into collaborative painting practices, yet hone in again on affective and sensational pedagogies (Ellsworth & Kruse, 2010; Massumi, 2002). In more praxic ways, this chapter privileges painting, a collaboration through an assemblage of the agency of non-human place, Art materials and objects, energies, affects, sensations, time, atmospheres, bodies, flows and other, and more-than-human worlds and worldings.

The processes again began at a writing retreat, for the Sustainability, the Environment and the Arts Research Cluster (SEAE), located at Southern Cross University, of which the authors are all members. We are artists, environmental educators, academics and PhD students – a collective of scholars. Our work is collaboratively and individually located in, with and around SEAE's mission, which is to enact profound change in/through transdisciplinary environmental and Arts education research that disrupts and generates new ways of becoming, and provokes dynamic responses to critical local-global calamities. We host writing retreats annually for SEAE members to gather and work collectively through environmental and Arts inquiry.

This latest retreat focused specifically on working the touchstones for socioecological learning from a previous collective publication by Cutter-Mackenzie-Knowles, Lasczik, Wilks, Logan, Turner and Boyd (2020) – itself the product of two previous writing retreats. Thus, with this chapter, we seek to stay with the emergence of the socioecological learner within a 'biosocial ecology of sensation' (Rousell et al., 2020) through the emergence of potentials for sensing, thinking, feeling, and learning. The departure in this chapter is the privileging of poetic image[1] and text, working the larval subject as an Arts-based experimental portrayal. For a more fulsome theoretical engagement, please refer to the original chapter. In this chapter, we begin with a distilling and then move onto the transformations of the larval subject, before closing with some final thoughts.

Distilling

Stretching further

following the processes of the wise.

The only rule is to experiment, to make, breaking all of the rules.

Pull everything out of failing,
creating then self-disciplined

in the analysis

leaving plenty of room for new rules next week.

Breaking all the rules, work it

find a place and
only make things

with people who do, work it.

Pull everything out, nothing is a mistake, it will lead to something,

and break all the rules.

If you work, *trust it*
trust the process, let go.

A mistake is just another experiment
If you experiment it will work.
All work is
experiment, in the making.
A larval subject, perpetually in the making, emergent.

Affective, sensorial, engaging
in, with and through
more-than-human-worlds.

Distillment

To distil socioecological learning, we embark on knowledge creation collaboratively (social) and situated (site) contextually (milieu). The experience of being situated in place enables learners to utilise the tools of sensation and the perspectives of others, to empathise, experiment and interact with the human and non-human, thus creating knowledge.

Knowledge is intrinsic in its creation through such extrinsic stimuli. This chapter artfully demonstrates how an individual's experience in a situated context can create knowledge as a result of engagement with/in social and individual socioecologies. Through engaging with the more than human in our collaborative artmaking we encountered materials: paint, dirt, water, forest, bugs, leaves, excessive heat and the humid air that joined with us in our image making. This image-text chapter, or visual essay, provides insight into the knowing and unknowing of the human and non-human (Rousell et al., 2020). This chapter artfully portrays the useful uniqueness of the bioecology, as the interaction between actors and milieu, which can shape and affect knowledge. As our collaborative Arts-practice-based-inquiry unfolded, we begin creating new sites/insights. This provided us again and again, during iteration after iteration, the evidence of a living breathing socioecology, live matter, the larval subject and the entwining of place (Irwin, 2013).

The site/sight/insight for this work is a property named Diptipur, situated in Northern New South Wales, Australia. It was originally built as a small family home, on farmland. Alongside the growing family, the rainforest has been replanted, and now covers what was once cleared paddocks.

Transformation 1: Laying the Ground

We walk, through the regenerated rainforest,

looking for a place, somewhere to lay the canvas.

We settle upon a bed of leaves.
They crunch and bunch the canvas.

The canvas feels foreign, a stark
white canvas set among the browns and greens of the leaf bed.

Hurrying to cover the white of the canvas,
using the leaves it rests upon to push and pull the paint.

Blue and yellow paint, the limited colours to which we have access, are
splashed across the canvas.

Adding water,
the paint, once thick and viscous, changes, and flows in rivers of colour:

merging.

Searching for something to hang our painting on, some nearby fencing, we find two pegs and watch the paint as it moves with a mind of its own, walking over the canvas, downwards. The canvas buckles under the weight of the paint and water. It seems out of place, a stark contrast to the surrounding muted colours of earth.

We leave the painting, waiting on the space to speak

Wind leaves, leaves and leaves:

watching, listening.

New word layering

The process
Colours
The process

Application

The process
Gravity, leaves, bugs
The process

Emergent. *Wait, until we meet again.*

Transformation 2: Hesitating Movement, Stillness, Evaluation (Adi)

It is morning and Katie has been down early to the work, adding another layer. I am excited to see what this is and how it will look. We arrive as a group and Lexi comments. We all agree that what Katie has done has changed it and made an immersive contribution to the next layer of paint. Katie talks about pulling it back, rather than putting more paint on.

I speak about my biggest challenge as an artist, which is to resolve work. The more I look at it, the more I think, maybe it's resolved already and then I start doubting myself. But it's not resolved. Lexi jumps in and starts grabbing handfuls of earth and starts rubbing it over the surface, adding a muddy hue. The dirt also acts as abrasion, pulling back more layers and revealing what's underneath. The performance of painting.

Transformation 3: The Third Return (David R)

Back in place, watching, listening, acknowledging the contribution of nature.

The process
Assessing
Time for more
The process

Finding, adding
Watching
Admiring the fearlessness of the evolution
Adding, scratching, revealing

The process
Assessing
Forwards and backwards moving
The process

Enough for now, until next time.

Transformation 4: Staying with the Trouble (Katie)

The painting troubles me. Weighs on my mind as I try to sleep. I wake and rush to layer again. To preserve some of the sections that speak to me. Haraway (2016, p. 1) speaks of trouble as a way to "stir up" and to quiet down aspects of life to create connections; to stay with the trouble so that we may be fully present.

I add white, pinks and purples. Circles from the lichen on the trees behind the canvas are reflected in the work. I am trying to breach the gap between the place and the forms on the canvas that seem so separate.

Again, I am drawn away, so it waits, still at odds with the surrounding place. The rain comes; it has been months since the earth has felt the drenching relief. My heart quickens as we are away from the work, and I wonder what effect the rain will have on the wet paint. The rain takes the paint on another walk and the paint continues to drip and flow. Yet, the painting is still foreign, contrasting with the place in which it sits, even as the elements have worked on it in our absence. We look together, we trouble, problem solve, and eventually Lexi grabs handfuls of dirt and leaves and starts scrubbing the painting.

... *aha*... this is *working*.

Transformation 5: Trying to Ease Trouble, But Trouble Troubles Us

A video of the process is freely available online at https://doi.org/10.6084/m9.figshare.19289636.v1

We scrub the work together, rubbing away at the top layers. The colours start to work, layers scrape away and the earth blends, a grid appearing from the fence the canvas leans on and hangs from. This is working. Finally, we are starting to see cohesion.

What is the Art? Is it the painting itself? Or is it also the reflections, the processes, the many layers as we build, and take away? Is it the relationship between our gaze and its surface? The intertextuality? Is it larval, is it emergent?

We walk – both in a physical sense, observing the site – and we walk with the painting, moving it to a new site/sight, as the paint walks across the canvas. "Walking is how most of us find our way in the world and as we do, we experience it in our own personal ways. Like walking, mapping is an embodied experience carried out from a particular point of view" (O'Rourke, 2013, p. XVII). Our minds walk as we move, as the painting moves, as the paint moves.

Transformation 6: A Cognitive Walk through the Methodology (Dave E)

As an artist who works with timber, my artmaking mainly involves a subtractive process. Cuts are carefully considered, the consequences are foreseen, and occasionally something to be feared. It is interesting to learn from others in a collaborative and experimental setting, where working with paint and canvas permits/encourages the artist to be brave in their making processes. I do wonder if this approach could be applied to timber in my individual making practices. What is it to be brave with timber?

I have been observing and enjoying the sedimentary process of painting in layers. What is interesting is the on-site/sight artists' assessment as well as the critical off-site collaborative rumination of the work. The processes of artmaking are not constrained to mere interaction with the canvas, as the socioecology can travel with the artist. Critical thinking can motivate the artist (Katie in the morning) to rush to interact with the work once more; or subdue the artists as they ruminate the next steps of the work and deal with their levels of contentment, or otherwise.

Using a socioecological lens that draws on the notions of the learner, the context and time (Cutter-Mackenzie-Knowles et al., 2020), the interactive processes and insight into making Art within a site/sight, result in a collaborative output that is unique, but not developed according to a planned schedule.

In this collaboration, time has provided the opportunity for the more-than-human to collaborate. Nature's contribution is seen in the action of forces that draw the paint downwards and outwards and across, and in the actions of the artists – human and more than human. Leaves and dirt pull the paint downwards and outwards. The wind and rain blow and spray, pushing the paint around. Soil, compost, leaves, and bugs are all in a constant state of movement and contribute to the work. Yet it is the drying processes of the sun that dictate when these processes are complete. Is this resolution?

Transformation 7: New Site/New Sight/Insight (Adi)

The work needs to move. We take it for a walk and re site/sight it.

Transformation 8: The Re/figure of the Socioecological Learner (Lexi)

Emerging through iterations
Re/sitings and re/sightings
Working in new site beginnings
Fresh colour, fresh ideas,
Form and structure re/shaping
Visual elements transforming, the learners
Re/sight, re/evaluate and re/iterate
Learners reshaping this c/a/r/tography
As embodied.
Collaboration: together/apart
We paint together, then apart,
think out loud together, and apart.

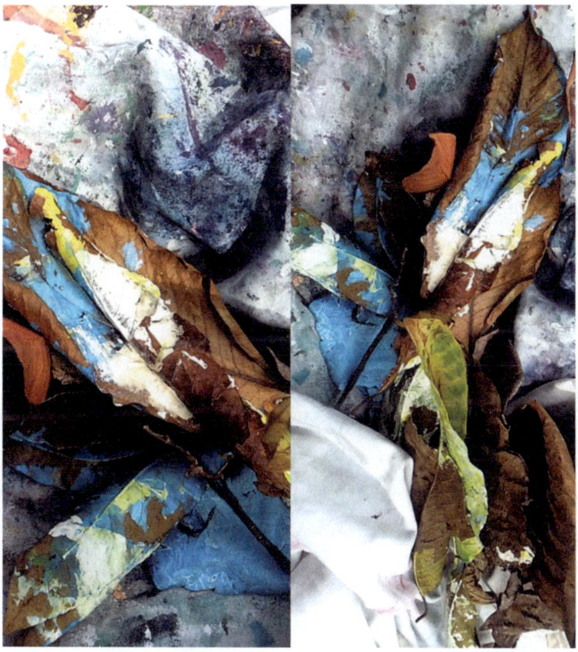

Transformation 9: Together/Apart

We write together, simultaneously, separated physically, but together in space, and thought. This collaboration, like the previous collaborative work, has become a breathing socioecology, a living inquiry (Irwin, 2004).

We are "inextricably entwined with place – the site/sight as ecology of sensation. It is this living engagement with site/sight as sensational milieu that forms the heart of our c/a/r/tography" too (Rousell et al., 2020, p. 11).

Transformation 10: Resolving Common Ground (Adi/Katie)

Adi

Five months later we come together again on common ground, at the university – working back into the paint.

It feels timeworn, dry, and inconsolable.

Coming from another time, a time of heat and humidity, transformed during seasonal change, when it was hot. It is not hot now.

Both Katie and I now find the dirt dirty and distasteful; it is winter. Should we remove it or let it stay?

Why not ask the dirt?

We do. The dirt does not want to go.

We work back into the paint using the same principle of common ground that we used this morning in another collaborative work. We make over, layer, scumble, tip and pour paint.

Paint, heat, water, dirt, push back, reaching to meet us halfway (Barad, 2007), resisting us, flowing on their own: paint painting, water painting, sunlight painting.

Katie

We let it dry and discover its new nuances. We are hesitant in our work together; I hold back, not willing to step on any ideas put forth by the other. As a result, the work went in directions that neither of us were happy with, but neither was willing to voice our unease in case we offended. Now, months later, we laugh, and commiserate in front of a work that neither of us love; indeed, we might hate it.

We set to work, trying to rescue a painting that went in a direction with which we are not happy. This time the painting pushes back at us, even as we try to fix it.

… maybe we fail.

Not only is the painting pushing back, but this time we resist each other. This causes a new tension to enter the paint, the canvas, and the ground. We push and pull against each other.

… failure is success.

Still unresolved; we leave, so the work can dry.

Transformation 11: The Final Returning (Lexi)

In the quiet of a morning when no one is around, I attach this errant painting to the glass wall and look. I look, knowing the others are struggling with it. The painting resists them, pushing back, pushing forward. Its emergence is resisted; it wants to remain larval, in process.

"You'll never resolve me", it mocks, in a whisper.

I pause. Reconsider. Become-with. Go. Follow the trails, the flows, the energy.

Speak, listen, attend. Work the passages, the silences and the bellowings. It's noisy, this painting, yet also strangely silent and uncooperative. It resists me too.

I listen to its stories, and I receive them, scratching and scratching with my pencils – 2 in each hand – then my brush barely loaded with white paint. Scumbling. Teasing it forward, pushing things back. The whoosh and the scratching of my gestures, a dance. Responding to the voices of it all, quietly adding my own. Becoming-with this painting in silence and in the voids and voices of time and place and energy.

Speaking back.

This larval entity emerges, relentless. There is beauty here, but it is in the detail, in the process, in its own becomings.

Paint runs and spools
Rivers made with yellow and blue
We chose our colours, we three
New collaborators, green

The paint sticks and slops
I feel warm breeze on my skin and in my clothes as sticky as paint
It is not cooling
It slops more sweat, viscous skin

Together we toil
Collaborators in socioecological learning
Sensing colour, texture, shape, and application
First pour, then fold paint over surface, the folder, the dirt

We make decisions together:
Shall we do this? I want to do that.

I'm just doing that now,
I silently ask the paint: What do you think paint?

The paint wants to paint
First our hands, maybe our feet
It moves slowly and thickly
The paint becomes our skin

Affected and infected
With entanglement
The materiality of the paint
Material to concept, we move again

Sometimes there are no decisions
Just the humble rhythm of instinctual movement
Our first layer, over layer, under layer
Is simply about the material

She comes back and tips the work some more
Dry leaves reach out for liquid drizzle
Again, we explore this embodied practice
Gestures of what is not yet known

Paint lends itself to an overspill
From the middle to the edges,
Working it, move it, running it
Dribble, dribble, slop, pour

We five becoming, as larval subjects
Always in process, being the process
Allowing the paint, ground, environment,
Leaves, air, sound, colour, humidity, heat, tools
to interpret us

This place offers us a site to become
Becoming-paint, becoming-liquid, becoming-growth
Working, the next layer is another growth
Embracing the moment
As the larval subject.

Closing

The self alone is never the expert. We learn this working together as the collaboration progresses temporally, physically and through relationality with human and the more-than-human. As artists, resourceful in practice, we work with nature and nature works with us by providing materials, atmospheres, milieux. Gershon (2009, p. XI) states that rewards can be found in creating space "for others to speak fully". These rewards are multilayered, as is the practice of painting. Perhaps our attempt to silence the dirt that kept returning was our way of preventing it from fully speaking – drowning it, covering it, and scratching it with the earth. Yet this painting was not drowned, not covered; rather it pushed back at us, asserting its agency, resisting us, until in the early morning quiet, it demonstrated its powerful aesthetic, drawing us into its details, its quiet moments of beauty and resolution. In this way the socioecology of painting, material, atmosphere, and the more-than-human is in socioecology with the human us. We reflect on 'our' (all of the 'our': human/posthuman/ more-than-human) collaboration as social relation, non-traditional and multidimensional (Gershon, 2009); indeed, as socioecological learning.

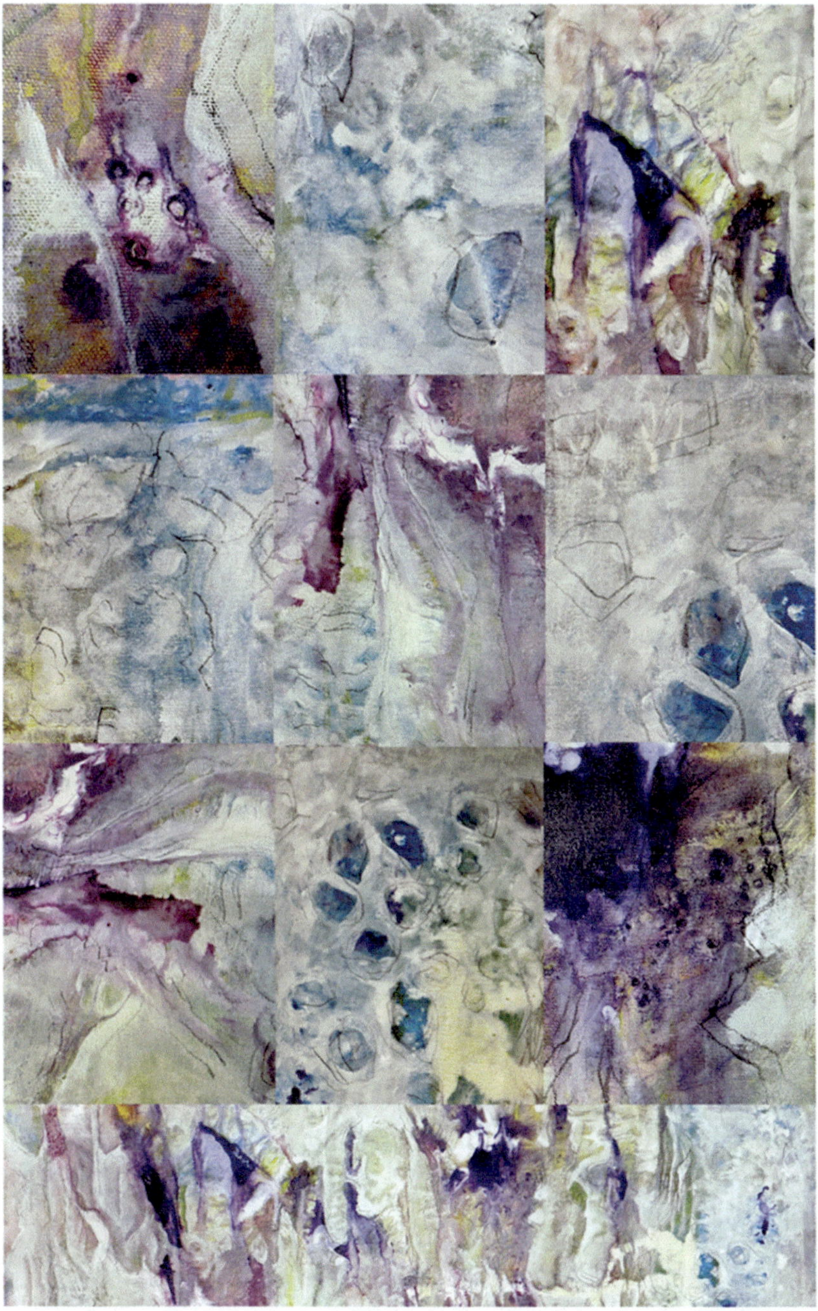

Note

1 The images in this chapter are not illustrations or figures and thus they are not labelled in such a way. Rather, they are critical texts in much the same way that the written text is. They are therefore meant to be considered and read as such.

References

Barad, K. (2007). *Meeting the universe halfway: Quantum physics and the entanglement of matter and meaning*. Duke University Press.

Cutter-Mackenzie, A., Lasczik, A., Wilks, J., Logan, M. R., Turner, A., & Boyd, W. (Eds.). (2020). *Touchstones for deterritorializing socioecological learning: The anthropocene worlds as creative milieux*. Palgrave Macmillan. https://doi.org/10.1007/978-3-030-12212-6

Ellsworth, E., & Kruse, J. (2010). *Touring the Nevada test site: Sensational public pedagogy*. Routledge.

Gershon, W. S. (2010). Entertaining ideas and embodied knowledge. In J. A. Sandlin, B. D. Schultz, & J. Burdick (Eds.), *Handbook of public pedagogy: Education and learning beyond schooling*. Routledge.

Haraway, D. J. (2016). *Staying with the trouble: Making kin in the Chthulucene*. Duke University Press.

Irwin, R. (2004). A/r/tography: A metonymic métissage. In R. Irwin & D. Cosson (Eds.), *A/r/tography: Rendering self through arts-based living inquiry* (pp. 27–40). Pacific Educational Press.

Irwin, R. (2013). Becoming a/r/tography. *Studies in Art Education, 54*(3), 198–215. https://doi.org/10.1080/00393541.2013.11518894

Lasczik Cutcher, A., & Irwin, R. L. (2018). *The flâneur and education research: A metaphor for knowing, being ethical and new data production*. Palgrave Macmillan.

Massumi, B. (2002). *Parables for the virtual: Movement, affect, sensation*. Duke University Press.

O'Rourke, K. (2013). *Walking and mapping: Artists as cartographers*. MIT Press.

Rousell, D., Lasczik, A., Irwin, R. L., Peisker, J., Ellis, D., & Hotko, K. (2020). Site/sight/insight: Becoming a socioecological learner through collaborative artmaking practices. In A. Cutter-Mackenzie-Knowles, A. Lasczik, J. Wilks, M. Logan, A. Turner, & W. Boyd (Eds.), *Touchstones for deterritorializing socioecological learning: The Anthropocene, posthumanism and common worlds as creative milieux* (pp. 49–74). Palgrave Macmillan.

CHAPTER 8

Playing with Posthumanism with/in/as/for Communities

Generative, Messy, Uncomfortable Thought Experiments

Maia Osborn and Helen Widdop Quinton

Abstract

Theorising to disrupt humancentric ways of knowing, doing and being is increasingly pursued in these eco-catastrophic times. Building on previous conceptualisations of human-non-human community learning, this chapter experiments with the practicalities of thinking and being with an entangled, beyond-human sense of community. The intention is to re-frame learning and being with/in/as/for all community. Posthuman concepts and perspectives are engaged with through multimodal, embodied, abstracted and layered thought experiments. By bringing ourselves as authors into purposeful, sensory, artful 'conversation' with the living and material co-dependents of our ecology, we experiment with ways of thinking and being in a world not centred on the human. Beyond-human physical and metaphorical experiences are entangled with body, self, other (human and non-human), concepts, place, space and time. These practices extend thinking, knowing, doing and being with/in/as/for community. Notably, these efforts unsettle our deeply held prejudices of being human that are difficult to detach from. These generative thought experiments reveal rich, embodied and creative ways of knowing and being, as well as provocations and tensions shared with the aim to spark beyond-human conversations with/in/as/for human-non-human socioecological learning communities.

Keywords

posthuman – more-than-human – community – Anthropocene – thought experiment

DOI:10.1163/9789004507838_009

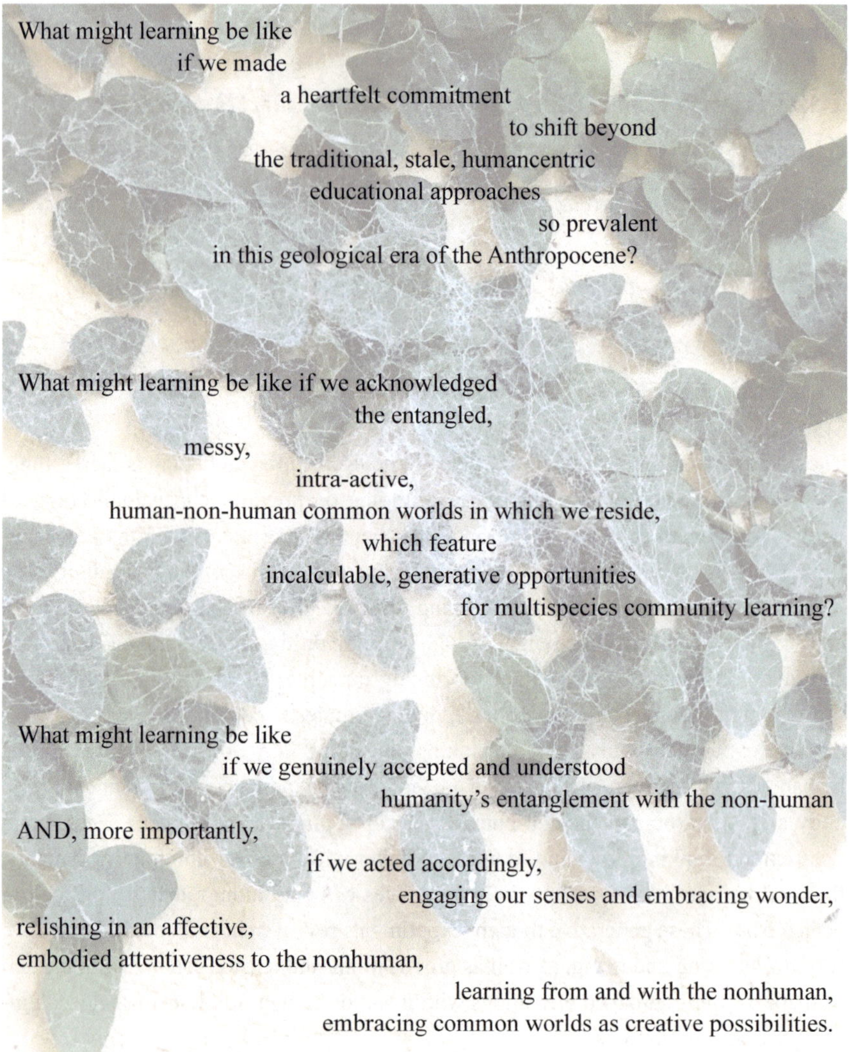
What might learning be like
if we made
a heartfelt commitment
to shift beyond
the traditional, stale, humancentric
educational approaches
so prevalent
in this geological era of the Anthropocene?

What might learning be like if we acknowledged
the entangled,
messy,
intra-active,
human-non-human common worlds in which we reside,
which feature
incalculable, generative opportunities
for multispecies community learning?

What might learning be like
if we genuinely accepted and understood
humanity's entanglement with the non-human
AND, more importantly,
if we acted accordingly,
engaging our senses and embracing wonder,
relishing in an affective,
embodied attentiveness to the nonhuman,
learning from and with the nonhuman,
embracing common worlds as creative possibilities.

Leveraging the Touchstones[1]

Pivoting from our interest in 'de-imagining[2] and re-invigorating learning with/in/as/for community, through self, other and place' that we have written about previously (Osborn et al., 2020), here we, the two authors of this chapter, experiment with arts-based approaches to imaginatively interpret what it means to learn and be with a beyond-human sense of community. Our intention is to encounter possibilities and complexities of common worlds community intra-actions in an exploratory and creative way. We pursue these aims via thought experiments, investigating “the nature of things” (Brown & Fehige, 2014, p. 1) through engaging our imaginations, senses and affect. In essence, these artful experimentations tease out human-non-human entangled experiences, beyond traditional academic or intellectual boundaries.

Launching from the ‘touchstone’ concepts of the Anthropocene, posthumanism and common worlds as creative milieux (Cutter-Mackenzie-Knowles et al., 2020) to de-imagine learning with/in/as/for community, we focus our orientation to engagement with the non-human essence and heart of community. In this era of human impacts on the Earth (the Anthropocene), our focus touchstones for reimagining generative intra-actions with common worlds of all beings and materials are posthumanism – regarding humans as just one of the many elements of the meshwork of life and matter – and creative meaning-making. Our immersion in the blurred, messy boundaries *between* human-nature, lively-inanimate and nature-culture focuses our attention upon possibilities of “fluid assemblages of human-non-human-place community encounters” (Osborn et al., 2020, p. 216).

In our efforts to de-imagine and reinvigorate learning with/in/as/for community, arts-based methods are placed into conversation with posthuman common worlding (Taylor, 2013), to practice being one among the many intra-acting (Barad, 2007) elements of community. We launch off our original chapter to engage in more “collaborative and relational research” that affords opportunities for human-non-human intra-action (Burke et al., 2017, p. 120). Taking a creative turn stretched our boundaries of comfort and experience, but allowed us to involve the sensuous and embodied, as well as the cognitive and affective – to engage with self-other-place in new ways. Our artful thought experiments are not aimed at creating art as a product, but rather as representations of making visible different ways of thinking and being. To engage differently through “unfamiliar experiences” that inspire “new conceptual and embodied frameworks” (Sayal-Bennett, 2018, para. 32).

These efforts constitute slow scholarship, commencing with an embodied immersion together in place, then independently and collaboratively re-engaging with place, artefacts, memories, reflections and imaginings, stretching over days and months for almost two years. Embracing slow scholarship and diverse experiences together and apart allowed us to move beyond linear conceptions of time and engage more fully with the “aesthetics of place, of experience, and of movement” (Lasczik Cutcher & Irwin, 2017, p. 117). Although we may have been ‘apart’ for some of this work in the traditional sense, our thinking, musing, pondering, learning, sharing and engagement with the non-human were always entangled and “entwined in myriad unfinished configurations of places, times, matters, meanings” (Haraway, 2016, p. 1).

Origins and Methods of Our Thought Experiments

Under the winding, whorling tendrils of a flourishing grapevine at a Sustainability, Environment and the Arts in Education (SEAE) Research Cluster writing retreat in 2019, we discussed the need to listen attentively to the non-human to inform and expand our understandings of community. Through thought experiments and embodied encounters, we sought to listen to and learn from the non-human – and ourselves – to distil what learning with/in/as/for community may look like, sound like, feel like, and what it has the potential to be/become within and beyond humancentric structures and contexts. We intended our thought experiments to constitute a liminal space between what is and what comes next – to inform the realisation of genuine human-non-human community learning. We hope our meanderings in this liminal space stimulate conversations, insights and ultimately, action. These efforts are motivated by a desire for greater, deeper and more widespread generative engagement with human-non-human communities to enrich learning, thinking, knowing, being and becoming in all facets of life – personal, community, society and beyond.

At the SEAE bushland retreat in the Northern Rivers of New South Wales, Australia, we commenced our first thought experiment by 'taking posthumanism for a walk'. We sought to purposefully decentre the human however we could, and therefore dwell differently in place. The non-human was honoured and valued through our committed attentiveness and sensorial attunement. Throughout this and the later thought experiments, we embraced "a radical openness to collaboration and encounter" with ourselves, each other, and the non-human, including place (Cutcher et al., 2015, p. 450).

We pursued a sensing, thinking, feeling awareness to the non-human as active agents in our encountering, learning, pondering, seeing anew. We walked slowly through the yard, gardens, buildings and bush; attentive to the position and movement of our bodies, other bodies and matter; listening, looking, feeling, smelling, touching. We strove to embody an awareness of our transcorporeality – deeply attuning to the intermeshing inseparability of human, place, other, and matter (Alaimo, 2010). We took considered photographs in the hope of eliciting insights into what non-human nature might be willing to share with us around learning with/in/as/for community. We were cognisant of the importance of "noticing, lingering, reflecting and trusting ourselves" to understand insights afforded by these creative, experimental acts (Lasczik Cutcher & Irwin, 2017, p. 118).

During this and later thought experiments, we documented our individual and shared experiences through a "performative process of walking and mapping" (Cutcher et al., 2015, p. 450). Specifically, we mapped these thought experiments and the liminal spaces between them through poetry, photography, mixed media collage, and slow conversation. Walking and mapping afford generative, creative opportunities for learning, research (Burke et al., 2017) and wayfinding (Lasczik Cutcher & Irwin, 2017). The entanglement of doing (walking) and recording (mapping) helped us to think deeply through, and simultaneously capture, these experiments. This enabled us to share the experiments with readers, to inspire continuing discussions around opportunities for posthuman community learning through deep and attentive sensorial engagement with the non-human. We see these efforts as both creative and theoretical work (Burke et al., 2017).

Being Common with/in/as/for Community: Thought Experiment 1

POSTHUMANISM
ANTHROPOCENE
CREATIVE MILIEUX
COMMON WORLDS

Thought Experiment 1 – Common worlding photo montage with images from the retreat on Bundjalung Country

gentle breeze, clean and green, warm embracing
shimmering
feeling, seeing, sensing
going deeper

invasion
resilience
clinging to the edge
micro mini - change direction
shift perspective
learning, growing
me, human
leaf, animal
rocks
heat
rain
renewing

hum/anim/all

Our efforts at common worlding through an immersive walk in the natural and built elements of community feel
clumsy
uncertain
uncomfortable
anthropocentric
not authentic.

Such challenges associated with thinking beyond humancentric boundaries are expected - because we are human! Our experiences mirror Prendergast's frustration – "I want to decentre myself, but I don't know how" (2020, p. 19). Like her, we acknowledge the limitations of language, and agree attempts to imagine ourselves as (or attempt to speak for) non-human beings "feels injurious/unjust" (p. 19).

Persisting, we explore further, dwelling and lingering with/in/as/for community.

Found Poetry from the Complexities of Our Research Stories[3]: Thought Experiment 2

Community partners facilitating learning
wandering
wondering and intra-acting with,
seeing

touching
sensing
feeling
appreciating the non-human
as "active communicating agents"[4]
ever entangled.

Embracing non-human nature as teacher who can
nurture
support
and share rich insights
with us.

Challenging the enduring silencing of the non-human
in education during the Anthropocene.[5]

Pushing the
boundaries of pedagogy
beyond the human.

Exploring the possibilities and potential of
what living *as* nature
truly means in *practice*.

Awareness of the sensitivities of the human body-as-nature,
porous and intermingling with other nature bodies.[6]

De-imagining community for parent and child,
where the human body-as-nature emerges
from a place of embodiment, a feeling,
rather than an intellectualising.

Engaging with/in/as the online space for
collective co-creation
social distribution of intelligence
knowledge production and meaning making.

Embracing collective socio-techno learning,
a complex intertwining biological and artificial
distributed intelligence

human and non-human.

Emplaced meaning-making, where
places *make* us.[7]

Intra-acting with the non-human,
we as mere parts of common world experiences
that influence and strengthen being and becoming in the world.
Unsettling traditional
rigid
human-centric classifications.

Opening up possibilities for
fluid assemblages of
human-non-human-place
community encounters.

Seeking possibilities for
learning how to unsettle,
rather than sustain
what is inherited[8] of the Anthropocene.

In this second thought experiment, Maia felt called to dwell with, reflect upon and see anew the four research stories from our original chapter (see Osborn et al., 2020). Inspired by Prendergast's (2020) evocative poetic conversation crafted from the work of Carl Leggo,[9] Maia revisited and 'mapped differently' our diverse ways of learning with/in/as/for community, by slowly and repeatedly being-with the research stories; reading, re-reading, mapping key concepts and ideas, before crafting a found poem.[10]

This process of experimentation – mapping through poetry – sought to play with the original chapter, re-interpreting the complexities and seeing anew the various possibilities for learning with/in/as/for community. The found poem illuminates precious gems in the original work, sharpening attention on key possibilities for human-non-human community learning with people, animals, farms, school grounds, gardens, community groups, businesses, online communities, human body-as-nature, and mountains. The poem is offered as a reminder of the diverse opportunities for human-non-human community learning that require urgent prioritisation in education and society more broadly, to respond to the challenges of this unsettling era – the Anthropocene.

Dwelling with Water Bodies: Thought Experiment 3

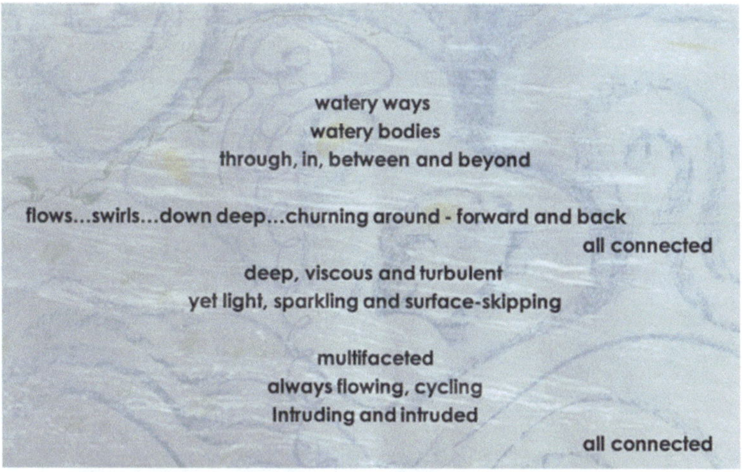
watery ways
watery bodies
through, in, between and beyond
flows...swirls...down deep...churning around - forward and back
all connected
deep, viscous and turbulent
yet light, sparkling and surface-skipping
multifaceted
always flowing, cycling
Intruding and intruded
all connected

Thought Experiment 3 – Encounter with watery bodies

In this third thought experiment, Helen sought new territory by dwelling with watery places through the lens of Neimanis' notion of porous bodies of water (2016), to think through intra-acting with the non-human community. By attuning to water flows in, around and through bodies, with sweeping, swirling marks on paper, a different level of entanglement with the meshwork of life and materials of our common world was felt, through embodied arts practices (Sayal-Bennett, 2018). Zooming into the microscopic movement of water molecules through clouds and leaf pores; the life-giving water flows of birth and living processes, with simultaneous sensing of being enmeshed in the macro scale movement of water that shapes the planet. All sensed through drawing movements and prose. In feeling and sensing the story of watery bodies, the logics of enmeshed bodies, places and matter emerged. With watery bodies concepts and arts-based deep thinking, common worlds connections through watery flows makes sense.

Slow Conversation Reflections on Human-Non-Human Community Encounters: Thought Experiment 4

Voice 1 (human element): *Experimenting with 'walking the talk' requires dwelling in the weave of the world without foregrounding human privilege. Purposefully disassociating from self as a bounded individual human was a struggle. But with stillness, attention shifts from the big human narratives of buildings and cut-down trees, to the quieter stories of water, birdsong, wind, warming sunshine, persistent plant growth and the industriousness of life all around. The listening with all of myself was an important learning – the embodied listening of the sensuous experiences, along with the deep listening to narratives that travel through and connect body-place-time into the different elements of local and planetary communities.*

Voice 2 (non-human community):

Thought experiment 4 – Slow conversation contribution 1 from non-human community at the retreat on Bundjalung Country

Voice 3 (human element): *Immersion with/in/as/for community through the camera lens in thought experiment 1 was initially a similarly-felt struggle, dominated by feelings of pressure – pressure to notice, photograph and learn from the non-human in a short space of time, within this constructed experience. The encounters with non-human nature felt somewhat artificial, ironically unnatural. But slowly, the agency of non-human matter – lively and inanimate – began to make itself known. The porosity and messiness of human-non-human boundaries emerged, as did a deeper awareness of my place within/as nature – just one part of a multiplicity of relational assemblages. As the pressure and concern to 'get it right' subsided, evidence of entanglement and non-human agency all around settled me into a slower, calmer state.*

Deeper understandings of time – specifically the entanglement of past-now-future – afforded insights and opportunities. Revisiting our encounters through artefacts and narratives, tangled with technology corruptions and the

limitations of language to portray embodied experiences enhanced appreciation of the agency of time. By slowing down, sensory attention became attuned to non-human agency to challenge binaries, blur boundaries, and experience a myriad of generative intra-actions with/in/as/for community. The importance of attuning to these intra-actions is the lesson that emerged most strongly through thought experiment 1.

Voice 1 (human element): *Taking time to be, know and act differently reveals the mismatch between human time scale and attention span with place and planetary time. First Nations peoples have long recognised the temporal weavings, foldings and unfoldings for being with/in/as/for community now often opaque to urban humans. Time dwelling with the non-human community through arts-based practices stimulated surprisingly deep engagement with the non-human community. Through these subtle, affective, sensory experiences, a glimmer of understanding emerged about the enduring entwinings of life and matter of community. Taking time and venturing into uncomfortable and uncertain territory of arts-based practices enabled entry into that liminal space between a humancentric perception of community and experiencing being with/in/as/for human-non-human community.*

Voice 2 (non-human community):

Thought experiment 4 – Slow conversation contribution 2 from non-human community at the retreat on Bundjalung Country

Voice 3 (human element): *These thought experiments strengthened intellectual and embodied understandings around the possibilities of slow, affective, thoughtful creative practices and pedagogies to inform and inspire both subtle and more radical conceptual, personal, environmental and social change. Creative pedagogies inspire a real depth of thinking, feeling, seeing, doing, knowing and being differently, by affording opportunities for wondering, listening, storying, imagining, embodying, enacting, experimenting, creating, negotiating, problem-solving, nurturing relationships, playing, singing, sharing, dancing, crafting (Ewing, 2020), learning, pondering, questioning, exploring, as well as expanding consciousness, understandings and sense of purpose. The process of engaging sensorially with non-human community brought surprises, particularly around the potential of arts-based experiments to generate deep insights.*

For example, the process of crafting the found poem served as a powerful lesson around the value of poetry as a genuine and generative research method. Through engaging slowly and thoughtfully with our previous research stories, attempting to distil the essence of the stories and share these insights creatively, understandings of the possibilities poetry presents in research were enriched. Poetry affords opportunities to get to the core of lessons learned through research and share these with a broader audience.

Furthermore, this slow conversation thought experiment inspired a deeper remembering of the retreat. Engaging more deeply with the experience, and then intra-acting with paper, scissors, glue and watercolours, artefacts, technology, place and non-human others to play again with efforts to attune to and sense entanglement with the non-human. Again, a sense of past-now-future as one emerged. This awareness prompted wondering differently, seeing differently, feeling differently, engaging differently (through memory) with the plants, animals, sky, soil, breeze, warmth of the sun, the agency of rocks, place, weather and an infinity of other non-human elements.

Memories surfaced of attunement to/with/as/for the non-human at the retreat, particularly the moment of experiencing a sense of breathing in and becoming-with the cosmos, while marvelling at the magnificent night sky. Through this opportunity to slow down with the cosmos, and engage with felt experiences, an even deeper awareness struck, viscerally. It was a powerful, embodied knowing of the environment not as a place, but as multiplicity of relational assemblages within which humanity is inextricably entangled, intermeshed and wholly dependent upon.

Voice 4 (materials and memories assemblage):

Thought experiment 4 – Slow encounter with non-human community: a materials and memories assemblage

Voice 1 (human element): *This slow encounter with materials and memories is such a vibrant recreation of the intra-acting community elements encountered in thought experiment 1. Our representations are, however, subjective human narratives. The images of non-human community as agential cuts into this slow conversation can only be anthropomorphising and interpreting non-human and material intersections with/in community. Nevertheless, these representations attend to and honour non-human voices, and model some strategies for meaning making about learning and being with/in/as/for community.*

Some Concluding Thoughts

Playing with posthumanism with/in/as/for community was a purposeful, artful venturing into new, and sometimes uncomfortable spaces. These experiments enabled dwelling in the messiness beyond humancentric community learning, involving encounters that were sometimes frustrating and unnerving, yet other times evoking a sense of ease, peace and togetherness. So, although fraught with tensions, taking posthumanism for a walk was nonetheless generative, and stimulated new possibilities for co-becoming with/in the common worlds, particularly through sensorial and creative efforts.

We therefore offer these thought experiments to stimulate and enrich awareness of humanity's entanglement with the non-human, and to inspire others to engage in posthuman ways of being, knowing and enacting learning with/in/as/for community. In essence, we sought to "somatically and relationally experience vibrations, perceptions and energies that flow, drift and emerge in, through, and with" creative, experimental acts such as photography, poetry and collage (Lasczik Cutcher & Irwin, 2017, p. 117).

So, in echoing Prendergast's query "What have I found in crafting this work, these poetic missives?" (2020, p. 31), we ask ourselves: What have we learned through engaging with these diverse thought experiments, dwelling with posthumanism literature, with the non-human in place, with entangled thoughts and ideas in multispecies common worlds? We have hinted at our learnings within the performance of our thought experiments, however, in the spirit of self-discovery and critical thinking, we wish to avoid stifling your own realisations with our potentially limiting reflections. It was not our intention to interpret or explicitly describe what the non-human was sharing with us, because everyone will engage with and learn from posthuman communities in different ways. Factors influencing our intra-actions with the non-human may include personal experiences, the local First Nations cultures and histories, our sense of place, and so much more.

Instead, we encourage the reader to now ponder what you have learned/ discovered/ realised/ found through engaging with this chapter. We invite you to pay particular attention to the insights you glean from the figures included in this chapter – our efforts to engage with the non-human creatively. We invite you to walk-with, think-with, know-with, be-with and become-with self-human-non-human-place communities moving forward. To discover and bring to life to creative common worlding in the Anthropocene. Finally, we offer some closing thoughts for the reader to linger with, to inspire reflection upon the possibilities of human-non-human community learning.

Seeking out powerful multispecies intra-actions
to generate
inspire
grow consciousness.

Pushing boundaries and unlearning limiting beliefs.

Ponder reflect
experiment play
learn discover
understand and see anew.

Embracing and illuminating the potential of
embodied
affective
sensory

human-non-human
community learning.

Situating/ positioning/ disrupting learning:
beyond the classroom, beyond the school,
beyond the human,
beyond the limitations of linear time.

Pursuing entangled human-non-human learning
to inspire engagement, understanding and meaning.

E x p a n d i n g perceptions of community learning,
heroing diverse, untraditional ways of learning in place,
embracing playfulness.

Reality, learning, education, absorbing, knowing, seeking is MESSY.

Dwell in and surrender to
the discomfort, the messiness, the tension, the struggle.

Learning is
inextricably grounded
with /in/as/for human-non-human communities.

Human-non-human community musings grounded in nature

Acknowledgements

We appreciate the support of the SEAE Research Cluster for providing the opportunity to collaborate through the 2019 Retreat. We also wish to express our appreciation to the anonymous reviewers and the editors, whose thoughtful recommendations guided development of this chapter. Our thanks also to Bryley Quinton for assistance with image design work.

Notes

1 The Touchstones are the four conceptual instruments from the companion book to the compendium this chapter is part of: Cutter-Mackenzie-Knowles, A., Lasczik, A., Wilks, J., Logan, M., Turner, A., & Boyd, W. (Eds.). (2020). *Touchstones for Deterritorializing Socioecological Learning: The Anthropocene, Posthumanism and Commonworlds as Creative Milieux*. Palgrave Macmillan.
2 As used in the companion book to this compendium of thought experiments, "'de' meaning 'from' in Spanish" (Cutter-Mackenzie-Knowles et al., 2020, p. 2).
3 Osborn et al. (2020, pp. 200–205).
4 Barrett et al. (2017, p. 132).
5 Barrett et al. (2017).
6 Malone (2018); Neimanis (2017).
7 Gruenewald (2003, p. 621, emphasis added).
8 Nxumalo (2017, p. 8).
9 Prendergast (2020).
10 In crafting the found poems at times Maia changed tense, added or removed words to improve flow, however the majority of words were found in, and borrowed directly from the original research stories, with permission from the authors (see Osborn et al., 2020, pp. 199–216).

References

Alaimo, S. (2010). *Bodily natures: Science, environment, and the material Self.* Indiana University Press.

Barad, K. (2007). *Meeting the universe halfway: Quantum physics and the entanglement of matter and meaning.* Duke University Press.

Barrett, M., Harmin, M., Maracle, B., Patterson, M., Thomson, C., Flowers, M., et al. (2017). Shifting relations with the more-than-human: Six threshold concepts for transformative sustainability learning. *Australian Journal of Environmental Education, 23*(1), 131–143. https://doi.org/10.1080/13504622.2015.1121378

Brown, J. R., & Fehige, Y. (1996/2019). Thought experiments. In *Stanford encyclopedia of philosophy*. https://plato.stanford.edu/entries/thought-experiment/

Burke, G., Lasczik Cutcher, A., Peterken, C., & Potts, M. (2017). Moments of (aha!) walking and encounter: Fluid intersections with place. *International Journal of Education through Art, 13*(1), 111–122.

Cutcher, A., Rousell, D., & Cutter-Mackenzie, A. (2015). Findings, windings and entwinings: Cartographies of collaborative walking and encounter. *International Journal of Education through Art, 11*(3), 449–458.

Cutter-Mackenzie-Knowles, A., Lasczik, A., Wilks, J., Logan, M., & Turner, A. (Eds.). (2020). *Touchstones for deterritorializing socioecological learning: The Anthropocene, posthumanism and commonworlds as creative milieux.* Palgrave Macmillan.

Ewing, R. (2020, July 16). *The imperative of creative pedagogies in contemporary teaching* [Online]. Dean's keynote, Southern Cross University.

Gruenewald, D. A. (2003). The best of both worlds: A critical pedagogy of place. *Educational Researcher, 32*(4), 3–12.

Haraway, D. J. (2016). *Staying with the trouble: Making kin in the Chthulucene.* Duke University Press.

Lasczik Cutcher, A., & Irwin, R. L. (2017). Walkings-through paint: A c/a/r/tography of slow scholarship. *Journal of Curriculum and Pedagogy, 14*(2), 116–124.

Malone, K. (2018). *Children in the Anthropocene: Rethinking sustainability and child friendliness in cities.* Palgrave Macmillan.

Neimanis, A. (2017). *Bodies of water: Posthuman feminist phenomenology.* Bloomsbury Academic.

Nxumalo, F. (2017). Geotheorizing mountain – Child relations within anthropogenic inheritances. *Children's Geographies, 15*(5), 1–12.

Osborn, M., Blom, S., Widdop Quinton, H., & Aguayo, C. (2020). De-imagining and reinvigorating learning with/in/as/for community, through self, other and place. In A. Cutter-Mackenzie-Knowles, A. Lasczik, J. Wilks, M. Logan, & A. Turner (Eds.), *Touchstones for deterritorializing socioecological learning: The Anthropocene, posthumanism and commonworlds as creative milieux.* Palgrave Macmillan.

Prendergast, M. (2020). Dwelling in the human/posthuman entanglement of poetic inquiry: Poetic missives to and from Carl Leggo. *Journal of the Canadian Association for Curriculum Studies, 17*(2), 13–33.

Rautio, P. (2013). Children who carry stones in their pockets: On autotelic material practices in everyday life. *Children's Geographies, 11*(4), 394–408.

Sayal-Bennett, A. (2018). Diffractive analysis: Embodied encounters in contemporary artistic video practice. *Tate Papers, 29*(Spring). Retrieved July 15, 2020, from https://www.tate.org.uk/research/publications/tate-papers/29/diffractive-analysis

Taylor, A. (2013). *Reconfiguring the natures of childhood.* Routledge.

CHAPTER 9

Agency, Power and Resistance from the Perspectives of All Beings

A Visual Ethnographic Inquiry

Marianne Logan, Thilinika Wijesinghe and Ferdousi Khatun

Abstract

This response is a creative and representation of socioecological learning through a posthuman framing. In order to facilitate environmental, ethical social and political change in a rapidly changing world we look beyond humans as being exceptional and 'saviours of the world', and encourage an awareness of the remarkable capabilities of other inhabitants of the Earth and the Earth itself. Agency, together with discourse, power and resistance are reimagined from the perspective of all beings. While immersed in the environmental crises that surround the Anthropocene Era, this response attempts to rethink the very concepts of 'nature' and the boundaries of 'human beings'. Rather than privileging ourselves as humans at the expense of all others we embrace the tangle of relationships in which we are enmeshed. We acknowledge and explore the power imbalance between humans, and between humans and all other inhabitants. This visual ethnographic interpretation is mapped out with concrete poetry, three-dimensional object photography, and narratives. This interpretation of the intricate loops and threads of its corresponding chapter endeavours to provoke thought and inspire agency and action with a diverse perspective.[1]

Keywords

posthuman – agency – power – discourse – resistance – Anthropocene

 | DOI:10.1163/9789004507838_010

Parched red soil (photo: Marianne Logan)

January/February 2019 /December 2019 /January 2020

Southern Hemisphere

Lines in the soil creeping, cracking, separating,
cool water that binds together
the tiny grains have vaporised in the heat;
dry, hard rocky soil, wreathing and opening up, movement … change.
January 2019 was drier than living memory,
leaves falling, plants limp, withering,
living things competing for water.
Australia is a land of droughts but this one is different,
it is the rainforest the cool, rich, forest, now so dry,
canopy opening as multitudes of leaves fall,
the sun's rays reaching the forest floor, dry,
flying foxes falling, dead on the ground from the heat in Victoria –
fires raging in Tasmania –
massive floods in Queensland.

Northern Hemisphere

people wake to the sound of cracking, exploding frost quakes,
the water in the soil snap freezing, expanding

soft moist soil, wreathing,
the splitting of the polar vortex dumping cold air
over Europe and North America.
Changing climate, changing weather,
the end of 2019–early 2020 – Australia burns, catastrophic, destruction:
The Anthropocene.

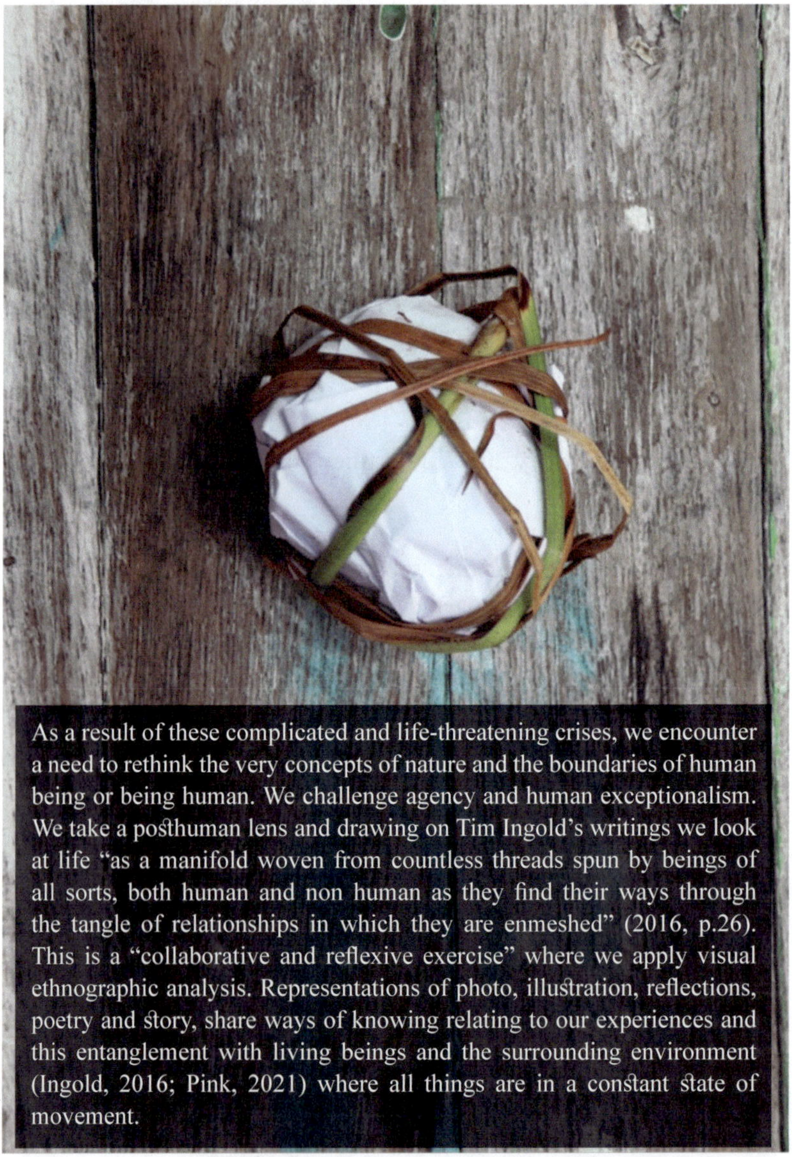
As a result of these complicated and life-threatening crises, we encounter a need to rethink the very concepts of nature and the boundaries of human being or being human. We challenge agency and human exceptionalism. We take a posthuman lens and drawing on Tim Ingold's writings we look at life "as a manifold woven from countless threads spun by beings of all sorts, both human and non human as they find their ways through the tangle of relationships in which they are enmeshed" (2016, p.26). This is a "collaborative and reflexive exercise" where we apply visual ethnographic analysis. Representations of photo, illustration, reflections, poetry and story, share ways of knowing relating to our experiences and this entanglement with living beings and the surrounding environment (Ingold, 2016; Pink, 2021) where all things are in a constant state of movement.

Assemblage. Photo: Marianne Logan; design: Thilinika Wijesinghe

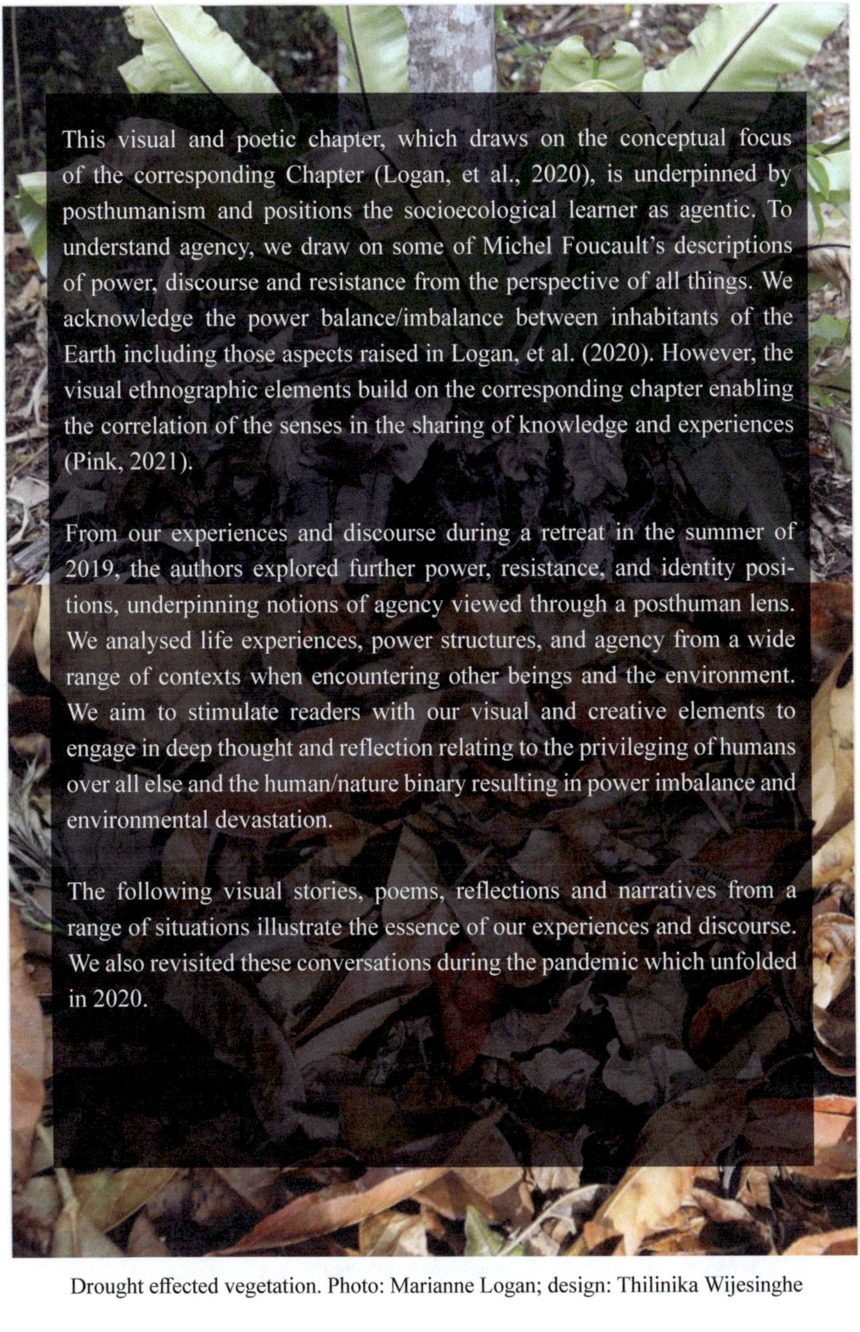

This visual and poetic chapter, which draws on the conceptual focus of the corresponding Chapter (Logan, et al., 2020), is underpinned by posthumanism and positions the socioecological learner as agentic. To understand agency, we draw on some of Michel Foucault's descriptions of power, discourse and resistance from the perspective of all things. We acknowledge the power balance/imbalance between inhabitants of the Earth including those aspects raised in Logan, et al. (2020). However, the visual ethnographic elements build on the corresponding chapter enabling the correlation of the senses in the sharing of knowledge and experiences (Pink, 2021).

From our experiences and discourse during a retreat in the summer of 2019, the authors explored further power, resistance, and identity positions, underpinning notions of agency viewed through a posthuman lens. We analysed life experiences, power structures, and agency from a wide range of contexts when encountering other beings and the environment. We aim to stimulate readers with our visual and creative elements to engage in deep thought and reflection relating to the privileging of humans over all else and the human/nature binary resulting in power imbalance and environmental devastation.

The following visual stories, poems, reflections and narratives from a range of situations illustrate the essence of our experiences and discourse. We also revisited these conversations during the pandemic which unfolded in 2020.

Drought effected vegetation. Photo: Marianne Logan; design: Thilinika Wijesinghe

Power and Identity:
Zoo time for the elephant's dance, performing dolphins, fish performances …
Overpowering the more than human for money making and human amusement.

They take – the oxygen, the shade, the food, the shelter and finally the timber – they dominate they burn, cut and destroy – we are there for their taking.

FIVE DOLLARS

Power and Identity:
They planted and nurtured me – I grow tall.

They perceive me as 'their object' that has grown as a result of their doing and they don't respect my power and identity. They take – the oxygen, the shade, the food, the shelter and finally the timber – they dominate they burn, cut and destroy – we are there for their taking.

Photo montage: Marianne Logan (for more additional information, see https://experimentingtouchstones.wordpress.com/)

The verve souls carry
when standing by a tree is
unique, rare,
strange (?).
The power lies within
the living being!
but how fickle, the
living being's power.
I question the norm
as I stroll
through
the walkway, the trees;
everywhere
seems to have
more power
than I do. I keep
wandering,
thinking, wondering,
thinking,
change is what we
wish for,
change is vital,
change is everything,
I look around for
change.
I see a climb at the end of
the dark chute
yet it seems so far;
so close yet we need
to get there
to be equal.

Ferdousi in the forest. Photo: Marianne Logan; design: Thilinika Wijesinghe

Fragmented forests,
Poaching, changing climate, degrading
landscapes, death,
destruction, multitudes of beings lost
forever,
palm oil, choices.
This entanglement of beings,
hands, hair, eyes, interwoven for one
moment in time, freedom for only one.[2]

Photo montage: Marianne Logan; design Thilinika Wijesinghe

Power is
fluid rather than
fixed; it can be positive
where it emboldens
action against ecological
and social injustices.[3]

Reflection (2018–2021)

This passage is an overview of the authors' reflections on the power of the youth-led climate change action movement and our belief that this initiative illustrates Foucault's notion of the fluid nature of power (Logan et al., 2020). Since 2018, young people from around the world, inspired by Greta Thunberg from Sweden, have been speaking out for action to address climate change and environmental devastation. These young people have carried out rallies and strikes, sometimes missing school to spread their message across the world (see image below). These actions demonstrate discourse, power, agency and resistance to address what they perceive as inaction by many governments to slow the progression of climate change.

In this example, young people have power to communicate with other, like-minded young people across the world through social media and discourse, which has led to action. This power, like Foucault (1980) asserts, is not power that is hostile or repressive; these young people are the vehicles of their own power, in order to influence governments and citizens, and in so doing demonstrate agency, resisting the call of many politicians to stay at school.

Young people are using their power and speaking out against a different type of power, one that is repressive and hostile, the human power behind the state of the Earth in the Anthropocene, accentuated by neoliberal governments advocating for economic growth at the expense of the health of the environment. This repressive human power is illustrated by the comments from an Australian Federal Government Minister, Matt Canavan, in response to the youth climate strikes. Canavan stated, "the best thing you learn by going to a protest is how to join the dole queue … I want kids to be at school to learn about how you build a mine, how you do geology, how you drill for oil and gas" (Australian Broadcasting Commission [ABC], 2018). This comment ignores scientific evidence that has demonstrated for decades that human actions, such as burning of oil, gas and coal, the clearing of natural habitats and the polluting of ecosystems, is leading to a changing climate and destruction of natural environments (Zalasiewicz et al., 2010).

Many young people who take part in these rallies are concerned about the state of the Earth and distrustful of governments who perpetuate repressive and hostile power towards the environment and are out of touch with young people. This concern is illustrated by the young people's slogans such as "the Earth doesn't belong to us, we belong to the Earth", "Governments lie, science doesn't", "Don't be a fossil fool" and "I speak for the trees, reef and fish" (see below).

In her speech to the United Nations Economic Summit in September 2019, Greta Thunberg told world leaders,

> You have stolen my dreams and my childhood with your empty words, how dare you … We are in the beginning of a mass extinction and all you can talk about is money and fairy tales of eternal economic growth … We will not let you get away with this … the eyes of all future generations are upon you, and if you choose to fail us, we will never forgive you. (ABC, 2019)

Following her speech, Greta Thunberg and fifteen other climate change activist youth filed a statement to the *United Nations Committee on the Rights of the*

Creatures NOT Cronies
DONT BE A FOSSIL FOOL!
GOVERNMENTS LIE... SCIENCE DOESN'T!
"UNLESS
"Someone like you cares a whole awful lot, nothing is going to get better It's NOT"
"I speak for the trees, reef and fish!"
The Earth Doesn't Belonge To Us We Belonge To THE EARTH
THERE IS NO Planet B

Climate Change Rally, Byron Bay Australia (photo montage: Marianne Logan)

Child stating that by failing to act on climate change world leaders had violated children's rights (ABC, 2019). Young people across the world have commanded respect and support as they engage in discourse and exhibit agency, power and resistance against environmental injustices. Many seek to emphasise the interconnection of all things, rather than the perception of the Earth as a resource for human profit.

The following narratives highlight the power and agency of other beings and the Earth and illustrate the interrelationship and entanglement of all things. The first narrative highlights the life changing experience of the second author, Thilinika, in relationship to agency and power of the environment and the second, the fear, suffering and enforced change, surrounding the power and agency of the global pandemic, COVID-19 by the third author, Ferdousi.

Narrative 1, 2004, Thili

Imagine yourself floating in the waters of the great Indian Ocean, on a warm boxing day in the year 2004. It certainly does trigger the mood for a holiday next to the beach. But what I am about to share is a not-so-pleasant experience of a 14-year-old girl whose life changed in a few hours, forever.

On Christmas Day 2014, my family and I drove to the Southern end of Sri Lanka to enjoy the sun, sea and sand of the coastal belt of the country. We were fortunate to be given a residential suite by a family friend of ours so we could spend the time luxuriously. After a scrumptious Christmas dinner, we returned to our rooms, which had fully upholstered four poster beds. It was as if we were camping in a jungle surrounded by the waters. Everything was to our hearts' content. We were delighted to be there and thankful for everything we had received. Hoping for finer moments the next day, we all fell into a deep sleep. This was a well-deserved holiday as we had all experienced a very busy year. As the surroundings were so very calm and quiet, we did fall asleep faster than usual.

The next morning, I remember opening my eyes, and when I opened up the curtains of the bed, all I could see was water and people, who were floating lifeless in the water, and houses flooded with water. Nearby a person was yelling for help trying to escape the floods. Having been a swimmer most of my life, I tried to reach out to this person who was struggling in the water without noticing what was going on. I stretched my right hand towards this middle-aged man, while grasping the bed post with my left. The further I reached the more I felt worried and something stopped me getting into the water. With the greatest difficulty, I was able to send a floating tyre towards the struggling man and he managed to grasp it, thankfully.

But wait! What's all this? Am I dreaming? I wiped my eyes and tried to call out to my parents. They were not in the vicinity. I saw some vehicles floating and moving around in the water. But what was all this water? I looked around and I realized I was in the Indian Ocean, floating on a four-poster bed – I felt like I was in a Disney movie. Five minutes passed. I continuously called out for help. I called out to my Mum and Dad, but there was no response.

After what seemed like hours but was approximately half an hour, I could see a speed boat hurrying towards my area, and I stood on the floating bed and waved at them to grab their attention. Finally, they spotted me and I found myself now in the drizzling rain on a speed boat with a team of lifesavers and a few others who were fully drenched in water, some who had lost consciousness and some crying and calling out.

It was utter chaos.

I asked one of the life savers what was happening, and he said the country had been hit by something called a 'T-sunami'. What on earth was this? I had never heard of a T-sunami. It took a couple of hours for me to realize that I had been a victim of an event that sometimes occurs in the world and I tried to familiarise myself with the term Tsunami, figuring out that the T was silent. The life-saver explained to me that a Tsunami occurs when there are earthquakes in the ocean and the water moves inland. This made me realize that I was a survivor of a catastrophic incident.

I don't know why I didn't wake when the Tsunami hit or how my bed came to be floating outside the house and what about my parents? I began to look for them. I, along with hundreds of others, was taken to a camp at a high location. There were many camps that had been set up and I walked into all of them looking for my parents. But no signs of them at all. Then I asked some military personnel if they had any information regarding my parents. By now, I could not hold myself back, and I broke into tears. I remember a kind-hearted lady walking up to me and saying, "Don't worry, your parents will come any minute", but, time passed by.

After 24 hours there was still no news of my parents. I was like a dead soul sitting in a corner, hoping my parents would return. A few hours later, I heard the voice of a military person saying, "there's another set of rescued groups coming in … get ready".

This gave me some hope. With the heaviest heart, I walked towards the gates of camp trying to see if my parents would be there. And yes – they were there! The kind of relief I felt, I've never experienced before or since.

My parents had been washed away to another area and they were stuck in that location, not being able to move, and the military rescuers had found them. My mother had panicked wondering where I was; I could see the deepest sigh of relief when she saw me. We returned home the next day with one of our relatives who had come in to check how we were.

But, there were thousands whose parents never came back, whose children never came back, whose friends never came back and whose pets never came back. This is when I learnt that the water had moved far inland, made worse by our clearing and manipulation of the natural coastline for building and construction. We don't realize how our actions can destroy natural habitats.

Humans might think that it is only they who have agency. What about the more-than-human others? What about the more-than-human things? In this case, the energy from the Earthquake in the depths of the ocean travelled through the ocean for kilometres resulting in this wild and furious uprising of water, causing massive destruction in many coastal areas in Sri-Lanka and other parts of Asia.

It took a Tsunami to change the way I looked at the world and my perceptions and views about the Earth and how my actions might impact others. I now acknowledge and respect the more-than-human others and the agency of all things.

Narrative 2, 2020, Ferdousi & Marianne

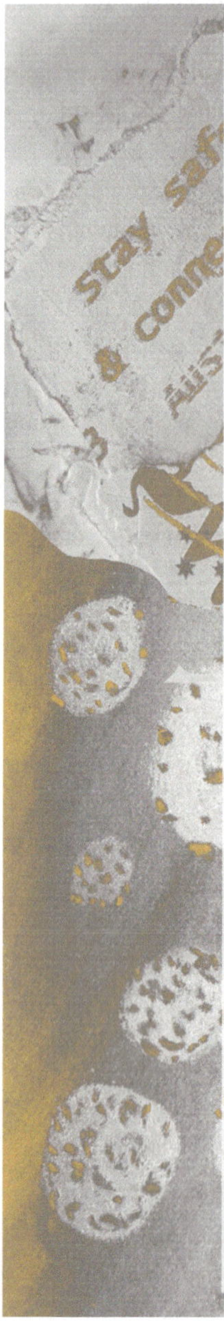

Lockdown in Dhaka, Bangladesh
I am confined to an apartment,
I use hand sanitiser,
disinfect door handles and the refrigerator,
and wash all groceries with warm water.
I go to the rooftop for sun,
I am lonely.

Lockdown in rural NSW
Confined to my home,
virtual communication,
I take solace in the forest, the trees,
The black cockatoos that fly over each day,
The echidnas under my house,
The microbats in the roof,
The sunrises and sunsets,
I miss family, my friends and my colleagues.

Humans have manipulated environments and changed the Earth,
but the power and agency of a tiny structure,
smaller than a bacterium, SARS CoV-2,
has humans at its mercy,
formidable,
only considered to be living when inside the cells of its host,
a genetic core wrapped in protein,
highjacking and programming human cells and replicating its genetic material (Ranasinghe, 2020),
cell to cell,
person to person,
town to town, and
country to country.
Proliferation, suffering, death and destruction,
invisible to us not knowing where it will emerge,
it has changed the lives of humans. Will this COVID-19 pandemic stimulate a rethinking of human exceptionalism?

Illustration and photograph by Marianne Logan; design by Thilinika Wijesinghe

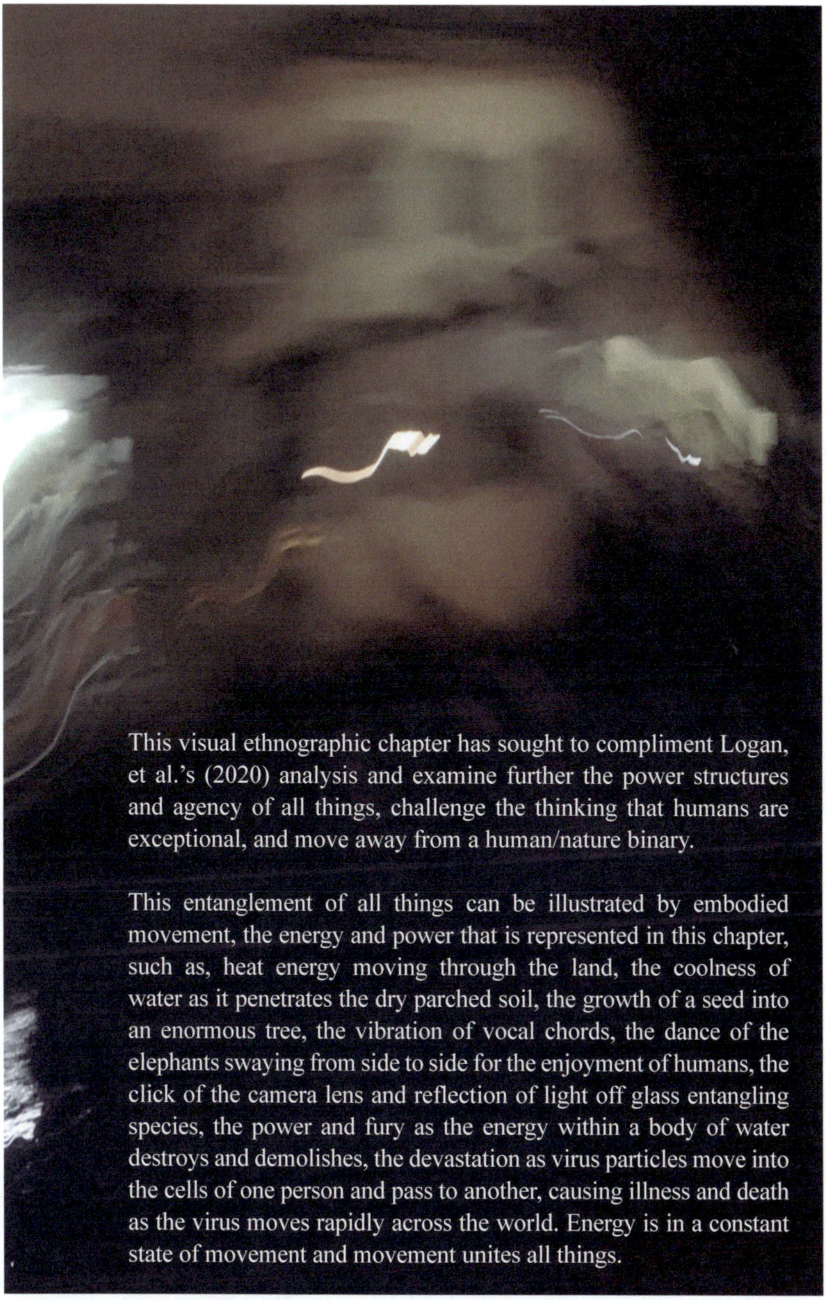

This visual ethnographic chapter has sought to compliment Logan, et al.'s (2020) analysis and examine further the power structures and agency of all things, challenge the thinking that humans are exceptional, and move away from a human/nature binary.

This entanglement of all things can be illustrated by embodied movement, the energy and power that is represented in this chapter, such as, heat energy moving through the land, the coolness of water as it penetrates the dry parched soil, the growth of a seed into an enormous tree, the vibration of vocal chords, the dance of the elephants swaying from side to side for the enjoyment of humans, the click of the camera lens and reflection of light off glass entangling species, the power and fury as the energy within a body of water destroys and demolishes, the devastation as virus particles move into the cells of one person and pass to another, causing illness and death as the virus moves rapidly across the world. Energy is in a constant state of movement and movement unites all things.

Photo: Marianne Logan; design by Thilinika Wijesinghe

Notes

1 The text is arranged in different sized columns to depict the inequality between humans and everything else.
2 Human/orangutan encounter/entanglement and associated power imbalances.
3 Foucault (as cited in Logan, Russell, & Khatun, 2020); Bazzul and Carter (2017).

References

Australian Broadcasting Commission (ABC). (2018). Students strike for climate change protests, defying calls to stay in school. *ABC News.* https://www.abc.net.au/news/2018-11-30/australian-students-climate-change-protest-scott-morrison/10571168

Australian Broadcasting Commission (ABC). (2019). Greta Thunberg joins climate change activists filing complaints at UN summit against carbon-pollution countries. *ABC News.* https://www.abc.net.au/news/2019-09-24/greta-thunberg-speech-climate-change-un-summit-how-dare-you/11541300

Bazzul, J., & Carter, L. (2017). (Re)considering Foucault for science education research: Considerations of truth, power and governance. *Cultural Studies of Science Education, 12*(2), 435–452.

Foucault, M. (1980). *Power/knowledge: Selected interviews and other writings, 1972–1977*. Pantheon.

Ingold, T. (2016). *Lines: A brief history*. Routledge.

Logan, M., Russell, J., & Khatun, F. (2020). Socioecological learners as agentic: A posthumanist perspective. In A. Cutter-Mackenzie, A. Lasczik, J. Wilks, M. Logan, A. Turner, & W. Boyd (Eds.), *Touchstones for deterritorializing socioecological learning: The Anthropocene, posthumanism and common worlds as creative milieux* (pp. 231–262). Palgrave Macmillan.

Pink, S. (2021). *Doing visual ethnography* (4th ed.). Sage.

Pitsoe, V., & Letseka, M. (2013). Foucault's discourse and power: Implications for instructionist classroom management. *Open Journal of Philosophy, 3*(1), 22–28.

Ranasinghe, K. (2020). How does a virus like COVID-19 spread? [Blog post]. https://blog.csiro.au/covid19-virus-spread/

Zalasiewicz, J., Williams, M., Steffen, W., & Crutzen, P. (2010). The new world of the Anthropocene. *Environmental Science & Technology, 44*(7), 2228–2231.

AFTERWORD

Entangled Found Poetry as Afterword

Alys Mendus

This afterword has been written through entangled found poetry, drawing on the work of Prendergast (2006, 2020), Leggo (2006) and Patrick (2016). As I read each chapter, made notes, mulled over the ideas and saw the 'gems' (Mendus, 2017, 2022) dancing around from MacLure's (2010) post-qualitative idea of 'data glow', I wondered, what was each chapter saying? Through further poetic inquiry and arts-based methodology I responded to the words in a poetic analysis of the experiences and scholarly work of the authors in this book: human, non-human and more than human, in a variety of poetic styles.

Each chapter in this book, was written collaboratively. So, I write this afterword collectively, with everyone in found poem tradition and I also write-with my colleagues from SEAE (Sustainability, the Environment and the Arts in Education Research Cluster) adding to this collection, an assemblage of entangled poems that open up the space for further de-learnings and de-imaginings of the socioecological learner.

1

We cannot
speak for the Earth,
BUT we can
trouble the tensions
having a conversation with
Matter, CHNOPS, Earth, Covid-19
And *linger in the act of writing.*
we are entwined, an assemblage of all things to have ever existed
chain-gang unique
COVID-19
'Civilisation' almost to its knees;
Stand still
Deep ecology at work
cataclysmic change.

 | DOI:10.1163/9789004507838_011

2

responding artfully to place
of the Arakwal people and
continuing sovereignty as Country of the Bundjalung Nation
Ephemeral events,
situated and experiential
documentation unavoidably incomplete,
Remembering we are nature
ghostly
tracings
linger
in these liminal spaces
as nomadic, always moving,
        inquiry into the not-yet-known.
Place-as-event is:
discovery and experimentation
constant movement, as the not-yet-known unfolds
acknowledging the entanglements
decentring humanism
troubling this tension
unsettling anthropocentric default perceptions.

3

Ghana:
the *Adinkra*.
symbols literally woven into the fabric
artefacts of Ghanaian culture
complex meanings, knowledge and wisdom
Mandala:
Creative messiness of lives and little things
Welcomes with equal warmth and measure
The poet and the mathematician
The storyteller and the scientist
Living breathes chaos and order just the same.
Interactions and intra-actions
Blur the lines and turn them inwards.
both-and-either-or-neither-nor and in-between.

Zygo – a symbol of peace
complicates
Curves
and multiplies linear representations
to make meaning of the wicked problems.
A material artefact
Of mental architecture
For creative and consilient explorations
of *Matter*, *Mind* and *Meaning* as different (*same*) dimensions of the same (*different*) thing.

4

pandemic closed schools

For a moment
There is space in the home-school day for exploration
To learn from outside
For risky socio-ecological learning
Mountain-bike; abseil; hike
There is
time in the day
to fail
to grow
to develop grit
'nature and children'.

pandemic parent-teachers
open schools to something new
'Risk' and 'failure' as generative-mechanisms
Shape the lives of the student-teenage-children
Confidently connect to capture 'risk'
In a deliberate space.

5

A world where learning is unbounded
The learner and the teacher are one,

Engaged,
Both their own person and integrated into a vortex
of common learning and knowing.

V O R T E X

We walk
We sketch,
We talk.
VORTEX VORTEX VORTEX

A future where categories are meaningless, individual ceases to dominate.
Flows from a mirrored honeycomb to an
interstitial space
VORTEX(T)

A curtain opening, a vision, an echo. Again.
Again.
Again.

6

J Journeying through Deep Time
O Opens **our road**, **our entangled story**.
U Utter quietness, *Universe flares,* unique
suspended infinitely in time.
R Re-imagine an interrelated and knotted world of future possibilities
N Navigates, new connections
E Encompassing space/deep-time interconnectedness
Y Years Morph, our future story.

E Engage metaphorically with echoes of Alice and her Wonderland
N Nature, non-living matter
T Transcend the inbetween, Transforming interrelationships with common worlds
A An a/r/tographical representation of Big History.
N Now,
G Gaze through the interactive lens
L Layers of intuitive understanding, Lingering in that moment,

listening to our beating hearts.
E *EveryThing* ***and*** *EveryOne!*
M MAGNIFICENT **Wonderland lies before us**
E Entangling past/present/future imaginings
N (u)Nfolding our complex universe, a
T Ticking clock of future possibilities
S Spacetime mattering
Dazzling our eyes!

7

Engaging with the more than human in our collaborative artmaking
We work with nature and nature works with us…materials, atmospheres, milieux.
Watch the paint as it moves with a mind of its own,
once thick and viscous,
changes, and flows
in rivers of colour:
Merging.

Grab handfuls of earth, rub over the surface
Breaking all the rules
This IS *humble rhythm of instinctual movement*
"OOH IT SMELLS DELICIOUS"
Dirt acts as abrasion,
"I JUST DON'T HAVE ENOUGH DIRT"
Pulling back more layers
The performance of painting.

But the painting troubles
on another walk
to flow
to ease trouble, but trouble troubles us.
The painting pushing back.
A new tension enters the paint
It resists
a breathing ecology,
a dance.
The larval entity emerges, relentless.

8

[redacted] learning [redacted]
a heartfelt [redacted]
[redacted] shift [redacted]
[redacted]
[redacted] entangled,
[redacted]
intra-active,
[redacted]
incalculable, [redacted]
[redacted] multispecies community [redacted]

Reimagining generative intra-actions with common worlds
Meshwork of life and matter
Apart-entangled-entwined
Whorling tendrils flourishing
Awareness
of our transcorporeality
our inseparability
Wayfinding.
hum/anim/all
The limitations of language with thinking beyond humancentric
Pushing pedagogy
De-imagining
Engaging with/in/as feeling,
places *make* us.
past-now-future as one.

9

Cool, rich rainforests
Now so dry

Fires raging
Australia burns.

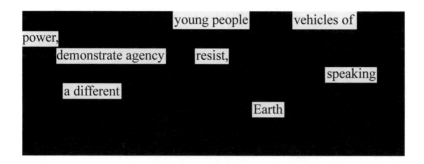

[redacted] young people [redacted] vehicles of
power, [redacted]
demonstrate agency [redacted] resist, [redacted]
speaking [redacted]
a different [redacted]
Earth [redacted]

Water, people, floating lifeless in the water
Tsunami

COVID-19
Lockdown, confined, virtual.
Devastation as a virus, virus as devastation
at its mercy,
all changing lives.

"We will not let you get away with this".

References

Leggo, C. (2016). A poem can: Poetic encounters. *LEARNing Landscapes*, *9*(2), 351–365.

MacLure, M. (2010). The offence of theory. *Journal of Education Policy, 25*, 277–286.

Mendus, A. (2017). *A rhizomatic edge-ucation: Searching for the Ideal School through School Tourism and performative autoethnographic-we'* [Doctoral dissertation]. University of Hull. https://hydra.hull.ac.uk/assets/hull:16594a/content

Mendus, A. (2022). *Searching for the ideal school around the world: School tourism and performative autoethnographic-we.* Brill.

Patrick, L. (2016). Found poetry: Creating space for imaginative arts-based literacy research writing. *Literacy Research: Theory, Method, and Practice*, *65*, 384–403.

Prendergast, M. (2006). Found poetry as literature review research poems on audience and performance. *Qualitative Inquiry, 12*(2), 369–388. doi:10.1177/1077800405284601

Prendergast, M. (2020). Dwelling in the human/posthuman entanglement of poetic inquiry: Poetic missives to and from Carl Leggo. *Journal of the Canadian Association for Curriculum Studies, 17*(2), 13–33.

Index

Printed in the United States
by Baker & Taylor Publisher Services